Making Livable Places

Transportation,

Preservation

and the

Limits of Growth

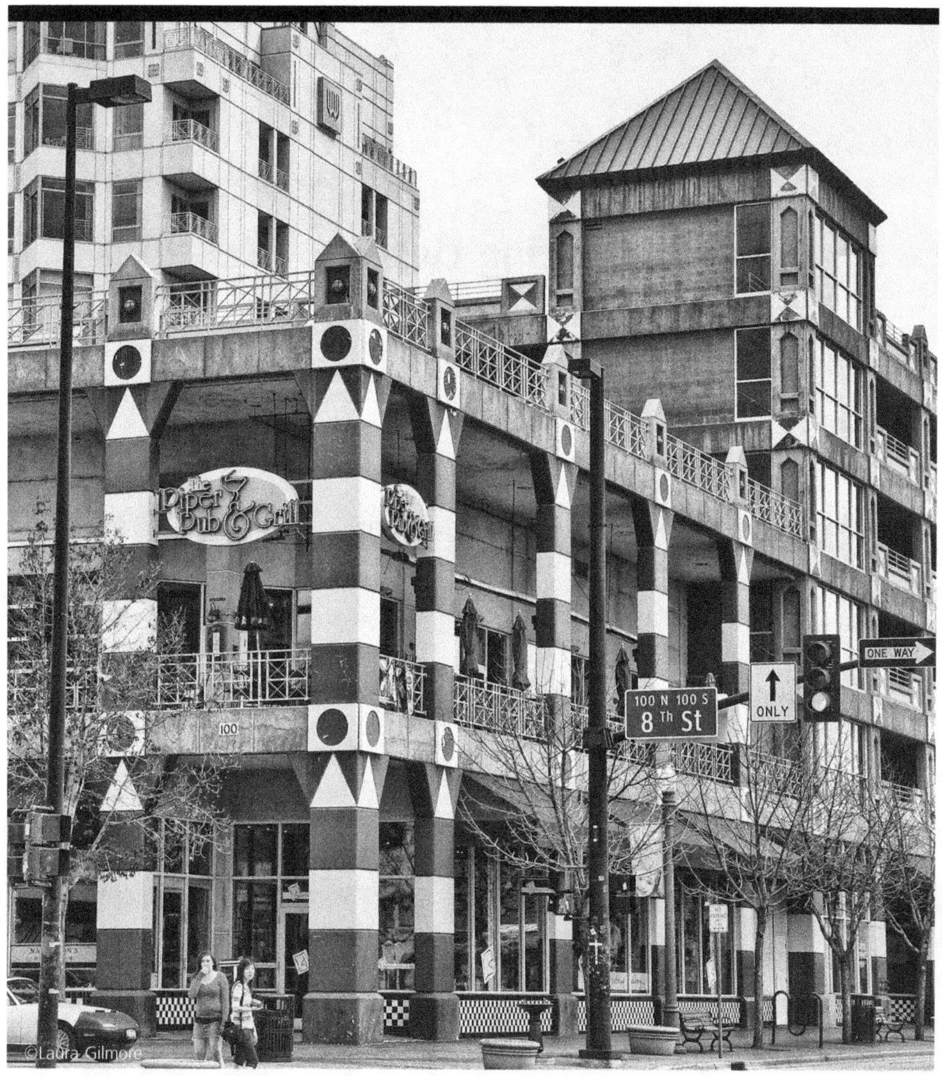

Eighth Street's Capitol Terrace wryly comments on the fantasy architecture of the 1927 Egyptian Theatre at Capitol and Main. Built by the Capital City Development Corporation (CCDC) in 1988, the parking structure rose from the sandstone ruins of Boise's largest department store.

making Livable PLACES

transportation
preservation
and the
limits of growth

Todd Shallat
David Eberle
Larry Burke, editors

Investigate Boise Student Research Series
Boise State University
College of Social Sciences and Public Affairs

2010

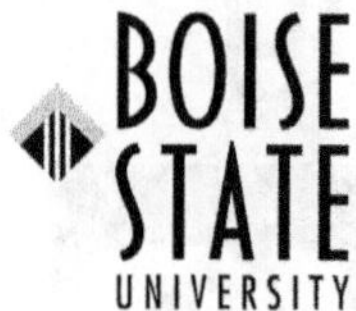

Todd Shallat, Ph.D.
Investigate Boise series editor
Center for Idaho History and Politics
tshalla@boisestate.edu

David Eberle, Ph.D.
consulting editor

Larry Burke
managing editor

Mary Harbst
student editor

Adele Thomsen
art director

Melissa Lavitt, Ph.D.
Dean, College of Social Sciences and Public Affairs

Boise State University
College of Social Sciences and Public Affairs
1910 University Drive - MS 1925
Boise, Idaho 83725

ISBN 978-0-557-32324-1

To order copies contact the
College of Social Sciences and Public Affairs at
sspadean@boisestate.edu

(208) 426-3776

The Investigate Boise Student Research Series ... the Boise State University College of Social Sciences and Public Affairs proudly sponsors a nine-credit field school for the study of the Treasure Valley. Each summer, about 40 students interact with professors, practitioners and public officials in a storefront classroom downtown. Students tour, investigate and compose documented research papers concerning political and social problems that vex municipal government. Top papers are peer-reviewed and edited for publication. Topics include housing and homelessness, neighborhood preservation, the political economy of energy and natural resources, and the challenge of urban renewal downtown. For information and sponsorship opportunities, contact Dean Melissa Lavitt at sspadean@boisestate.edu; (208) 426-3776.

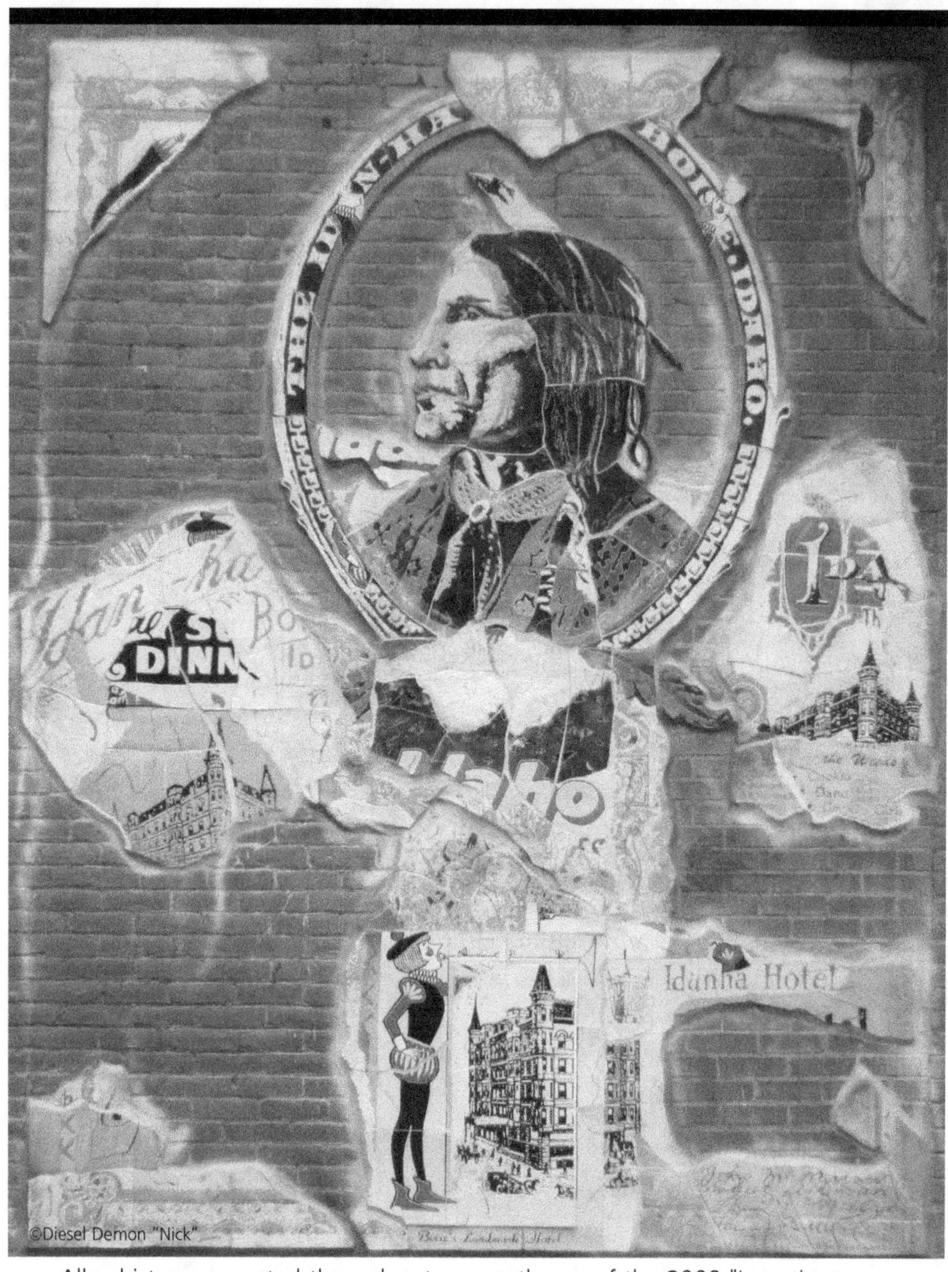

Alley history presented through art was a theme of the 2009 "Investigate Boise" field school on urban affairs. Pictured: Kerry Moosman's 2001 tribute to the Idanha Hotel.

Contents

Introduction

Making *Livable Places* explores the history and politics of the issues and places that shape Boise's metropolitan growth. In the summer of 2009, in the donated space of a vacant downtown storefront, the investigation began as a Boise State University field school on urban affairs. About 40 students attended. City planners and elected officials worked with professors from five academic departments. There were architecture walks and visits to blighted places. There were bus and Segway tours. Students wrote research papers, and 11 were selected for publication by the Boise State University College of Social Sciences and Public Affairs.

The approach has sometimes been called place-based education. Holistic and experiential, it makes the city a living textbook. In June, our summer began with the downtown core of Boise. In July, we broadened the lesson to the Boise Valley and the city's role as regional hub. Students selected from a list of research topics concerning transportation, preservation, conservation, housing, homelessness, crime, regional planning and urban renewal. Professors Todd Shallat and David Eberle invited top students to continue for additional credits. Eight students were recruited from the summer program

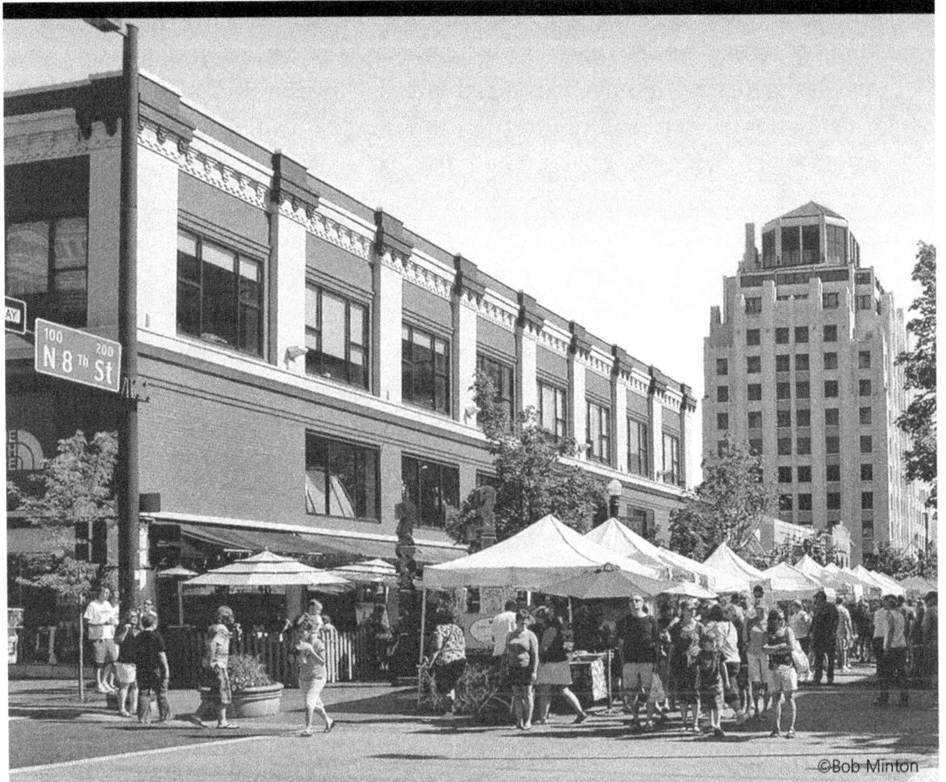

"Investigate Boise" thrived in the donated space of a storefront classroom. Pictured: Boise's Capital City Public Market at Idaho and Eighth.

and three were master's students who had previously written on Boise topics. Under the guidance of editor Larry Burke, the student authors stepped through the process of publication—of revising, fact-checking, documenting, editing, graphics selection and book production. The result is an anthology of essays on urban issues that vex municipal policymakers. It showcases the pragmatic application of social science research to the study of public affairs.

Students were asked to place local problems in historical context—to understand the origins of disputes, to appreciate how recurrent historical themes shape decision-making today. Chris Mansayon's study of the Boise streetcar, our lead essay, illustrates the importance of historical context.

Mansayon returns to a city of risk-taking entrepreneurs in an era when power grids and rail lines were powerful tools of economic development. Ann Felton's essay on a threatened Eighth Street warehouse also explores the importance of railroads. Felton gets to the nub at what is at stake in the preservationist's fight to keep historic streetscapes whole.

Even in places without iconic historical landmarks, preservation can contribute to economic development. William Blackadar's essay on Collister follows a neighborhood that emerged from an orchard on an electric street-car line. Collister's revival depends in part on promoting neighborhood identi-ty. Ted Vanegas tells a similar story in a study of the suburbanization that transformed the Ustick townsite. Both essays begin with the streetcar. Both offer hope that walkable streets and traffic-calming improvements can help neighborhoods prosper and grow.

Student historian Jacey Brain studies planning and livable places through the tight lens of a single downtown corner. Ever since the Boise gold rush, Eighth and Idaho has always been a commercial hub. City Hall once anchored the corner, which later became ground zero for the razing of historic buildings during the era of urban renewal. Today a mix of historic uses—of retail, cafes, offices and nearby workforce housing—contributes to the urban feeling that helps downtown commerce survive. Some of the elements that have allowed downtown to prosper are evident through the camera lens of Leo J. "Scoop" Leeburn. A photographer of fires, crime scenes and stories for the *Idaho Statesman*, Leeburn documented the demolition of historic brownstones during urban renewal. Student historian Mary Harbst provides a sampling of Leeburn's photography with an emphasis on the city that Boiseans lost.

Sarah Cunningham's essay on the Central Bench studies the connection between history and revitalization, between the need for historic centers and the future of a place overwhelmed by the automobile. Shaded sidewalks, better lighting, bike paths and landscaping can make the area more inviting. A emerging "international district" of immigrant markets and shops may help the neighborhood prosper by nurturing a new sense of its place.

While Boiseans debate the revitalization of auto-dependent strip malls, planners lay the foundation for a network of high-speed buses. Student investigator Kelly Foster provides a revealing interview with Kathleen Lacey, a city planner. Buses, Foster explains, are gaining popularity. But an effective alternative to auto commuting may require funding in the form of a local option tax. Bus rapid transit may also require stronger cooperation among the dozens of jurisdictions that compete for highway funds.

Central to the campaign for better transportation is the problem of urban sprawl. Planners agree that smaller houses closer to downtown Boise can alleviate traffic congestion. Houses far from the workplace add commuters to the highways, pave farmland, cripple wildlife and foul the valley's dirty air. Sprawl pits conservationists against developers and property owners. Tedd Thompson marks the lines of dispute in an essay concerning the The Cliffs, once a planned community approved on a foothills plateau called Hammer Flat until the City of Boise purchased the land. Kurtis Hawkins looks at the Avimor development between Boise and Horseshoe Bend. Both authors emphasize urban impact areas and the limits of a city's power to contain developments outside their boundaries.

David Webb concludes with strategies that a city such as Boise might use to preserve livable places. The list of "smart growth" tactics includes zoning reform, landmark preservation, the reinvestment in vacant buildings, workforce housing, buses, light rail and land-use policies that reduce the dependence on cars. Smart growth begins, says Webb, with public education about the ramifications of development policies. Webb's plea for education about the dynamics of cities resonates with the College of Social Sciences and Public Affairs. Our mission, simply stated, is to train informed citizens, and to clarify the confusion that clouds voting and policymaking. We proudly submit these essays as proof that place-based urban research can help Boise grow in a responsible way.

Todd Shallat, Ph.D., directs the Center for Idaho History and Politics at Boise State University. His Boise writings include *Ethnic Landmarks: Ten Historic Places that Define the City of Trees* (2007).

David Eberle, Ph.D., serves on Boise City Council and the board of directors for the Capital City Development Corporation (CCDC). He specializes in tax-financing, transportation and urban renewal.

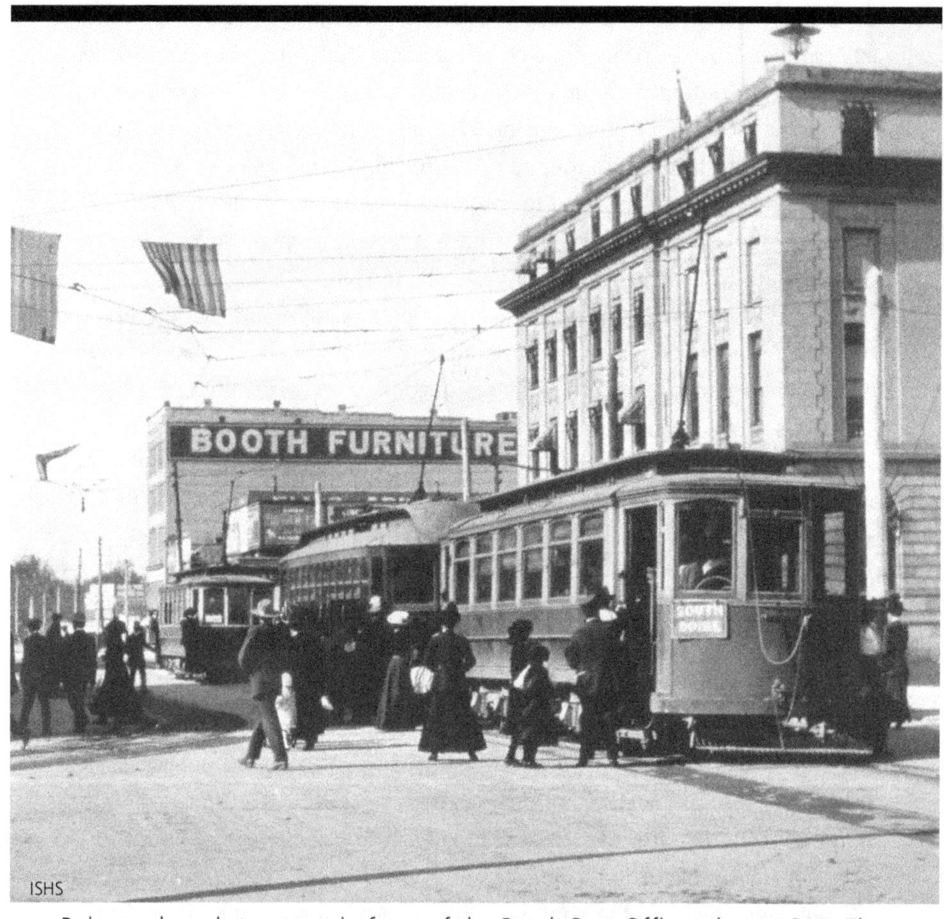

Boiseans board streetcars in front of the Borah Post Office, about 1915. The Borah building faced the main trolley depot at Bannock and Seventh.

Boise builds a
STREETCAR

by Chris Mansayon

While federal funding for a proposed downtown streetcar loop didn't materialize, the need for enhanced mass transit will remain high on the agenda as city leaders work toward solutions to more effectively move people into and around Boise's downtown core. Whether the proposed 15-block east-west loop through downtown or another route is eventually selected, the return of the streetcar appears to be only a matter of time—and money. As novel as the concept seems today, the current discussion over streetcars takes a page from a 110-year distant past, from a time when streetcar routes played a key role in shaping Boise's first neighborhoods, connected the city's core to the surrounding countryside and linked all of the communities in the valley. Perhaps a look at how streetcars benefited Boise in the past can provide some perspective on the future.

It is hard to imagine that the character of present-day Boise was shaped by something that existed a century ago—and is now extinct. Today, few residents remember an era when they could board a rail line in Boise and travel to Caldwell, Eagle or Nampa, or when farmers from Ustick and Collister used the Interurban streetcar line to ship goods to Boise. Even Boise's famous North End was originally created and shaped to be a street-car suburb. For those who lived during the peak of the streetcar age, trolleys must have seemed as new and magical as the mysterious electricity that powered both them and the city. Will the streetcar in Boise work its magic once again in the second decade of the 21st century? That is a question yet to be answered. But there is no question that Boise's streetcar system was a magic potion when it spurred the region's development more than a century ago.

In 1869, the first transcontinental railroad connected the nation, effectively shrinking the United States. Long gone were the days of six-month wagon trips from Missouri to Oregon. Most of the nation could now be traversed in as little as a week. Just a few years after such a monumental achievement, steam cars were being seriously considered as a mode of interurban transportation to link nearby towns together and provide a faster mode of transit than walking, horse-driven carriages or horse cars, which were trolley cars and trams pulled by animals on steel tracks. But the noise and smoke of steam power was impractical, so most American inventors turned their efforts toward other forms of motion and the steam-powered trolley eventually went on to enjoy far greater support in Europe and Australia. Cable cars seemed to be a more practical substitute, but that technology also was short-lived. Only San Francisco and a few other cities held onto their old cable car systems. By the time the 1900s rolled around, many major cities were turning to new electric trolleys. Boise was one of the early adopters, establishing the first lines in 1891, only three years after Frank Sprague had completed his first electric system in Richmond, Va., and just four years after Boise first received electricity. Chartered in 1890, the Boise Rapid Transit Company (BRTC) laid down 2.25 miles of track between 14th and Idaho streets and continuing down Warm Springs to the newly constructed Natatorium. The two companies in charge of the electric lines and the construction of the Natatorium even coordinated their efforts to draw people onto the streetcars and provide them an easy way to get to the Natatorium pool. Like many of the early lines, the Warm Springs line was a great success, boosting migration to the area and promoting development east along Warm Springs Avenue and as far south as the Boise Bench. At the request of several prominent Boiseans, by 1900 plans were drawn up to take the first steps toward the creation of an interurban rail system by expanding the trolley system outside the city limits. In 1904, the BRTC's first rival, the Boise and Interurban Company (B&I), was created and charged with the construction of a new electric rail line to connect Boise and Caldwell. Plans were immediately drawn up and tracks were laid following the same lines that

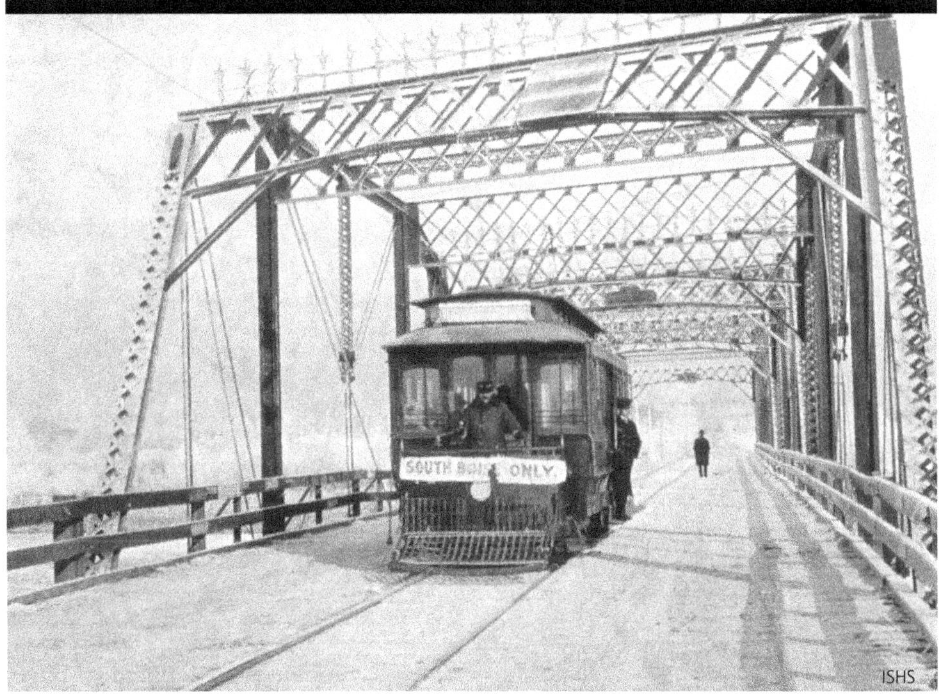

Streetcars connected the City of Boise to the independent village of South Boise via the Broadway Bridge, about 1910.

State Street and Highway 44 now occupy, passing through Eagle, Star and Middleton before heading south to Caldwell, ending where the iconic Saratoga Hotel stood until 1990.

At the same time the B&I began construction on its stretch of line, a third company, called the Boise Valley (Electric) Railroad (BVRR), received permission to begin working on a project of its own. Starting from within Boise at Broadway, going to Morris Hill and extending out from Fairview Hill, the BVRR laid tracks westward along Fairview Road until jutting north at Cole, following Ustick Road and eventually stopping at Meridian and Nampa. By 1912, the BVRR owned 31 miles of track, had 21 cars in operation and was the Boise Rapid Transit Company's main rival. The independence of the three competing companies was to be short-lived and by 1912 they were merged

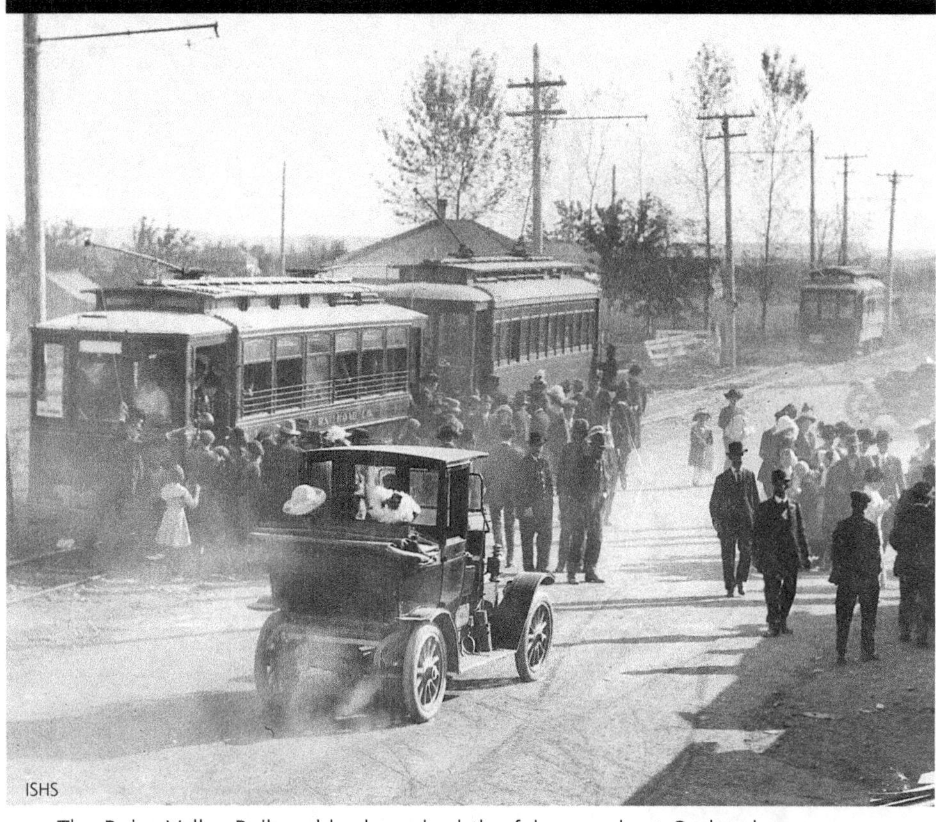

ISHS

The Boise Valley Railroad had reached the fairgrounds at Orchard near Fairview by 1905. A funeral car extended the line to the city's cemetery at Morris Hill.

into one large corporation named the Idaho Traction Company. The consolidation of the three companies was immediately beneficial to the traveling public and shortly after the merger a new segment of tracks was laid between Nampa and Caldwell, connecting the two former rival lines of the BVRR and the B&I into one large loop that spanned more than 60 miles after completion. New stops were also added in the farmlands to accommodate the people who lived away from population centers. The new enclosed trolley cars carried people and their goods at speeds reaching more than 50 miles per hour. Not only was the new "Boise Valley Loop" a popular Sunday excursion, but just like Warm Springs, property values along or near the line skyrocketed and new developments sprung up seemingly overnight, allowing the ITC to boast more than 70 stops along the line at its peak of operation. Country depots were also informal communal hubs and farmers often set up produce shops near the trolley stops to sell and transport their goods all across the valley. These small towns, which constituted the majority of stops between larger hubs of Boise, Meridian, Nampa and Caldwell, earned the nickname of "Toonervilles" for the name of the clanging or "toon" sound that came from a trolley as it was about to arrive at a stop. In addition to a small station that resembled a modern sheltered bus stop, Toonervilles usually consisted of only a small grocer's store and a crossroad. The nickname was also given to country residents by upper class city dwellers and urbanites, but as the larger towns expanded and distinctions between town and country disappeared, so did the nickname.

Trolleys ran quickly between stops and during the early years of operation a trip anywhere on the rail line cost just 5 cents. After a few years, a trip to most places still cost a nickel but longer rides, such as the weekend excursions families took along the Loop, might cost up to a $1.50. On a clear day, an entire trip around the valley took roughly two hours, with each trolley making between 50-70 stops for passengers and freight. The Boise and Interurban line highlighted stops at the Natatorium and Pierce Park, which were visited far more frequently than other attractions in the valley. After lines had been connected to Caldwell in 1907, promotional travel rates were given to patrons who were going to the Canyon County Fair. Through the years, the trolley cars created a way for people to connect with one another and were a unifying force within the Treasure Valley.

Popularity would not swing the way of the streetcar forever. By the time the Idaho Traction Company emerged in 1912, the automobile was winning over newspaper headlines throughout America for its low price tag and potentially lower maintenance costs. Before 1910, the privileged could be seen driving up and down Warm Springs Avenue and the popularity of the new mode of transportation steadily grew over the next 10 years. The costs of WWI temporarily stalled the fall of the American streetcar. Passenger traffic actually rose during that time, but that only put off the inevitable. New "trackless trolleys" began to emerge and slowly replaced the increasingly expensive and aging streetcars. The entire nation slowly succumbed to this new trend, with only a few cities hanging on to their old urban and interurban lines. In Idaho, the Idaho Traction Company was divided into the Boise Streetcar Co. and the Boise Valley Traction Co. in 1915, and the two firms returned to their old ways of competing with each other. The upper hand eventually went to the Boise Streetcar Co. in the 1920s when it began switching all the trolleys out for new, gas-powered buses. The switch, combined with the growing popularity of the automobile, prompted many cities to begin large paving projects, further drawing away profits from the Boise Valley Traction Company, which had to cut back on car maintenance in order to cope.

Finally, on May 17, 1928, with work already underway on a new, state-of-the-art highway between Nampa and Boise, the Interurban system shut down all passenger and freight service indefinitely. The last streetcars unceremoniously ran the last routes of the Loop and at 6 p.m. they were all shuffled into barns and passengers were handed bus schedules. The closure of the Boise Valley Traction Company met with strong opinions on both sides. Farmers and businessmen who relied on the routes protested the loss of the system, while many citizens who no longer used it praised the notion that they would never have to hear the screeching of the railcars again. Newspaper headlines boldly proclaimed that during its last few years of service, the Boise Traction Company had gone $2 million into debt and that in September of 1925, a foreclosure suit had already been filed on the dwindling company. Bondholders split up and bought portions of the lines, which were all eventually removed or paved over to accommodate growing automotive and bus traffic. For Boise, and much of the rest of the United States, the magical age of electricity and the street rail was over in a flash.

With the exception of an occasional lament over the lost trolley car or a reminder of the "good old days" by an Idaho newspaper whenever old lines are dug up to repave an existing road, little attention is given to the old system in the age of the auto and "super highways." Occasional *Idaho Statesman* articles give readers cause to reminisce about Boise's long lost trolley car system, which was hastily buried underneath new road developments. Titles like "Remember? Buried rails recall a bygone era" or "Newfangled streetcars found popularity quickly in Boise" graced the paper as people began to realize that no matter how large the freeways and roads were, or how many lanes wide they were, that they would never solve the problems of congestion alone.

Perhaps the most noticeable reminder of Boise's streetcar legacy is a restaurant aptly named "The Trolley House" located on Warm Springs Avenue. Originally built in 1922, the building served as a dispatch station at the east end of a line that ran as far west as Eagle and Star. This building in particular was constructed so people could visit the area's largest attraction, the Natatorium. The only indication of the building's former use is a large mural painted on the western wall depicting a red trolley car with several

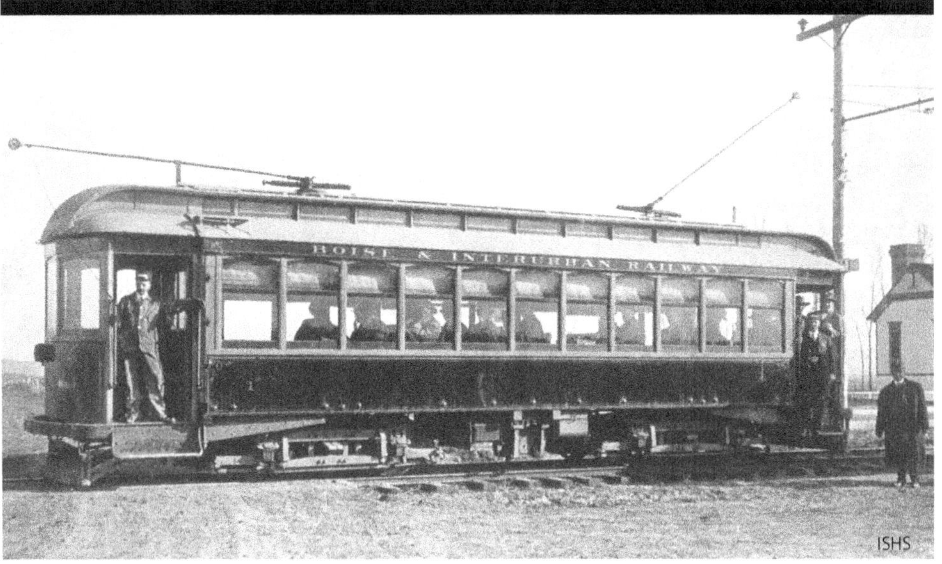

The Boise and Interurban Company extended its line from Main Street to Caldwell along Valley Road (now State Street). In 1912 the B&I merged with its rivals to create the Idaho Traction Company.

passengers on board. Inside, the walls are adorned with pictures, newspaper clippings, photos and other various crafts contained within display cases. Another remnant once nestled in the Boise Bench neighborhood at Rose Hill and Roosevelt. The "Trolley Bar" began life as a train car in 1882, serving as both a passenger car and a caboose for the Oregon and Washington Railway & Navigation Co. before being rebuilt in 1911 to serve as a trolley car in downtown Boise. In 1930, it was retired and moved to Rose Hill to become an ice cream parlor before finally being converted into a local tavern in 1934, where it became one of the longest running businesses in Boise. All that came to an end in 2006 when the Trolley was partially burned in an arson fire, subsequently forcing the owner to board up its doors and shut down. Restoration estimates have ranged anywhere between $10–40,000 depending on the scope of reconstruction.

The last 20 years have seen the successful reintegration of the trolley car into urban transit systems as cities have realized that highways alone are not sufficient to move masses of people from growing suburbs to the urban

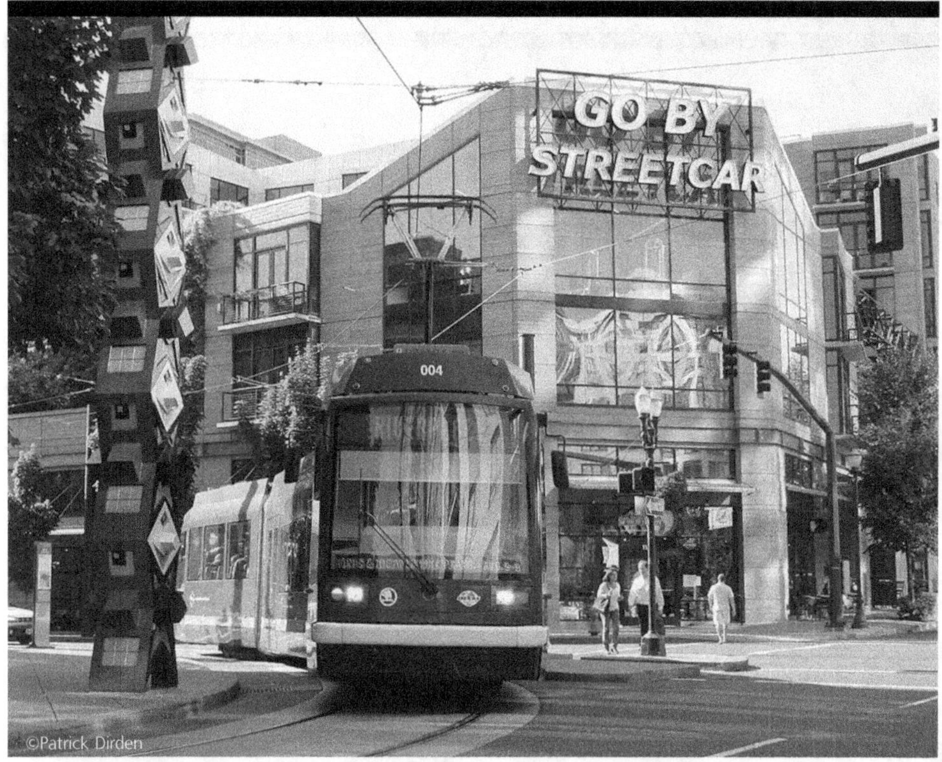

Portland's streetcar has inspired a controversial campaign to rebuild Boise's system as an economic development tool. Pictured: Portland's Pearl District.

core. San Diego began building a new system in the 1980s. Denver also revitalized its streetcar system as a light rail system in 1994. Many major cities quickly followed suit and either recreated, or in the case of Boston and San Francisco, renovated and expanded their still-existing systems into popular and invaluable assets to the communities they serve. One of Boise's closest sister cities in the west, Portland, entered its second age of light rail in 1986 under the direction of the Tri-County Metropolitan Transportation District of Oregon. Between 2001–05 alone the interurban rail system produced more than $2.3 billion worth of urban development. More than 30 cities in the

U.S. and Canada currently have a streetcar or light rail system, or both, and more than 80 cities either have plans or have begun construction on new streetcar systems, including Washington D.C.

Some local leaders and business owners are saying that now it is Boise's turn. In 2004 various proponents from the local and state levels came together and created what they called the "Boise Mobility Study" in order to determine the growth needs of downtown Boise. The study concluded that the development of a new form of transit to serve the downtown sector was much more desirable than widening streets to accommodate more traffic. Two years later, the Treasure Valley High Capacity Transit Study examined how to successfully integrate a new transportation system that would not only include downtown Boise, but also eventually connect the major Treasure Valley communities back together; streetcars were the answer. They also concluded that a downtown system would not only enhance the transportation system, but also help revitalize underdeveloped areas served by the streetcar route. As a result, the downtown streetcar proposal came to the fore. The project didn't clear its first financial hurdle and is back on the drawing board. But the streetcar emerged as a major player in the mass transit discussion. Will there someday be a new valley "loop" that extends to Star, Emmett and Kuna? Will the old headline, "Valley Once Had Trolley Line," someday be replaced with, "Valley Once Again Has Trolley Line"? Time can only tell.

• • •

Chris Mansayon is a senior who will graduate in spring 2010 with a major in history and a minor in Chinese culture. A 2005 Kuna High School graduate, he plans to pursue a master's in applied historical research or library science.

What are the most important aspects of a "livable" city?

"The most important aspect is planning, planning, planning. Not just selfish planning for 'us' and 'right now,' but planning for 10, 15, or 20 years down the road. It would greatly serve our community to take the time and MONEY (I know this state hates spending money) to do it properly the first time around rather than rush to employ patch solutions."

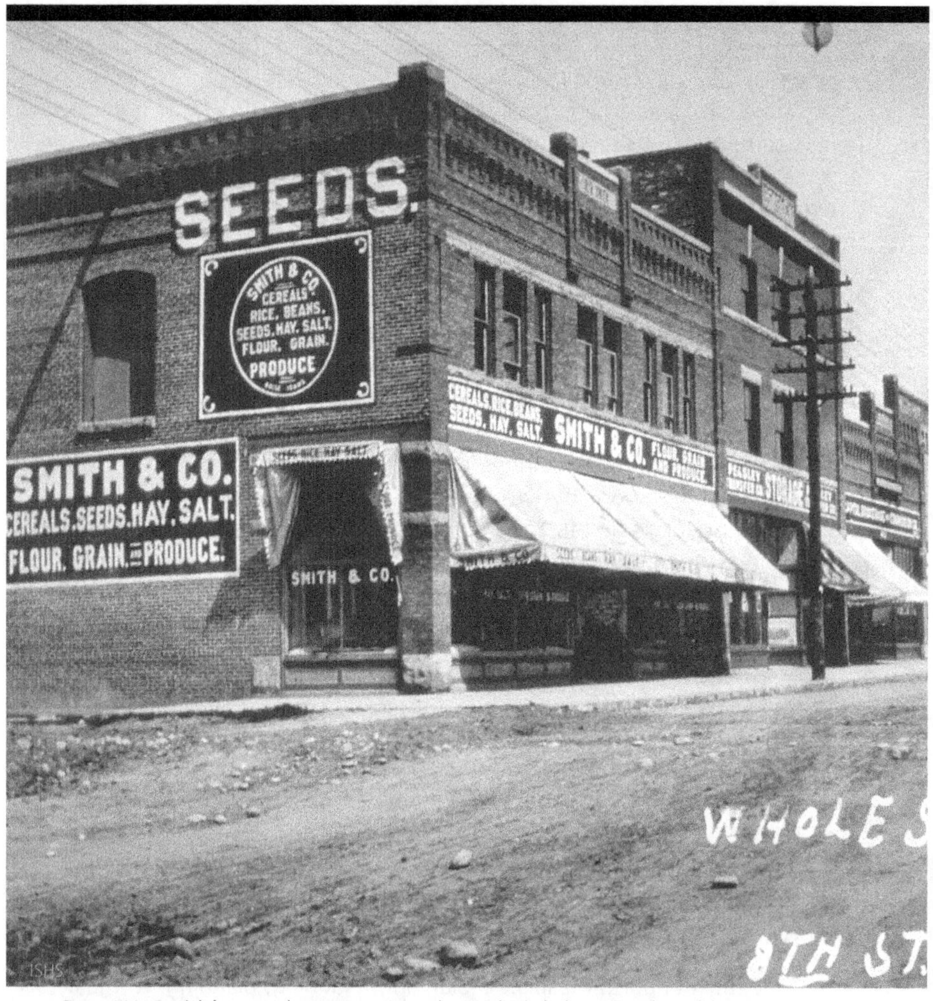

Otto W. Smith's warehouse at Myrtle and Eighth, completed in 1902.
Pulleys and hoists unloaded goods from wagons on the building's
south side.

Saving the
WAREHOUSE

by Ann Felton

O n Aug.1, 1864, Boise teamed with activity as 100 immigrant wagons streamed down its crowded Main Street, mixing with those of local farmers bringing hay and produce to market. Adding to the confusion were long lines of ox teams loaded with lumber and other goods from Salt Lake and the Columbia River. Scenes such as these are far removed from today's growing metropolitan area of Boise. The last visual images of that time in history disappeared in 2006-07 with the reconstruction of the O.W. Smith Building, the oldest building in the downtown warehouse district. Its reconstruction took away the bay windows and doors that serviced the freight wagons of pioneer Boise. This destruction of the city's past might not seem so surprising except that it occurred in a designated historic district supposedly designed to protect historically significant buildings. With this development came questions about the city's commitment to preserving a sense of its historic past.

As with most towns, Boise's battle to preserve its heritage has evolved over the last 60 years. After World War II the city grew as the nation prospered and the GI Bill created new suburbs throughout the surrounding bench areas. Businesses in the core of the city started to suffer as small neighborhood malls appeared in the outlying developments. In 1965, city leaders followed the nationwide trend of renewal and redevelopment in hopes of transforming Idaho's capital city into a modern and viable business center. They created the Boise Redevelopment Agency and a plan evolved calling for the replacement of the "deteriorating downtown core" with a new open-air mall. Soon blocks of older buildings were bought and demolished using federal funds from the U. S. Department of Housing and Urban Development. What the city didn't realize was that many of those old and deteriorating buildings contained a cultural and historic connection to the citizens of the town. As people started to see their heritage piled high in rubble, some started to question the demolition. When the bulldozers started to approach the iconic 1927 Egyptian Theater, people stood up to fight against the eradication of their past. But only after blocks of historic structures had been razed did they stop the destruction that had engulfed many pioneer buildings as well as what was left of a once thriving Chinatown.

Across the nation, communities started to question the practices of those early urban renewal efforts and in the late 1970s President Jimmy Carter authorized a series of tax breaks for those engaged in historic preservation. This change in policy hit Boise at a time when a lack of financial backing had ground the downtown mall project to a halt. Suddenly, enterprising businessmen started to look at those "deteriorating buildings" in a new light and together with innovative architects began to refurbish the historic fabric of the downtown area. The city recognized there was value in promoting the cultural history of Boise. In 1976, the city established the Historic Preservation Commission with a mandate to "promote, preserve and protect historic buildings, structures, sites, monuments, streets, squares and neighborhoods" so they could serve as a visual reminder of the city's past. Through the creation of historic districts, the commission could designate areas that held special historic significance to the city and then exercise an oversight position over reconstruction of visual elements in those areas. All major remodeling or construction projects in those districts had to pass the review of this commission and its decisions could be overturned only by the City Council. During this time, what had once been a struggle between developers and historic preservationists turned into a win-win situation with the refurbishing of old structures into productive commercial spaces. In

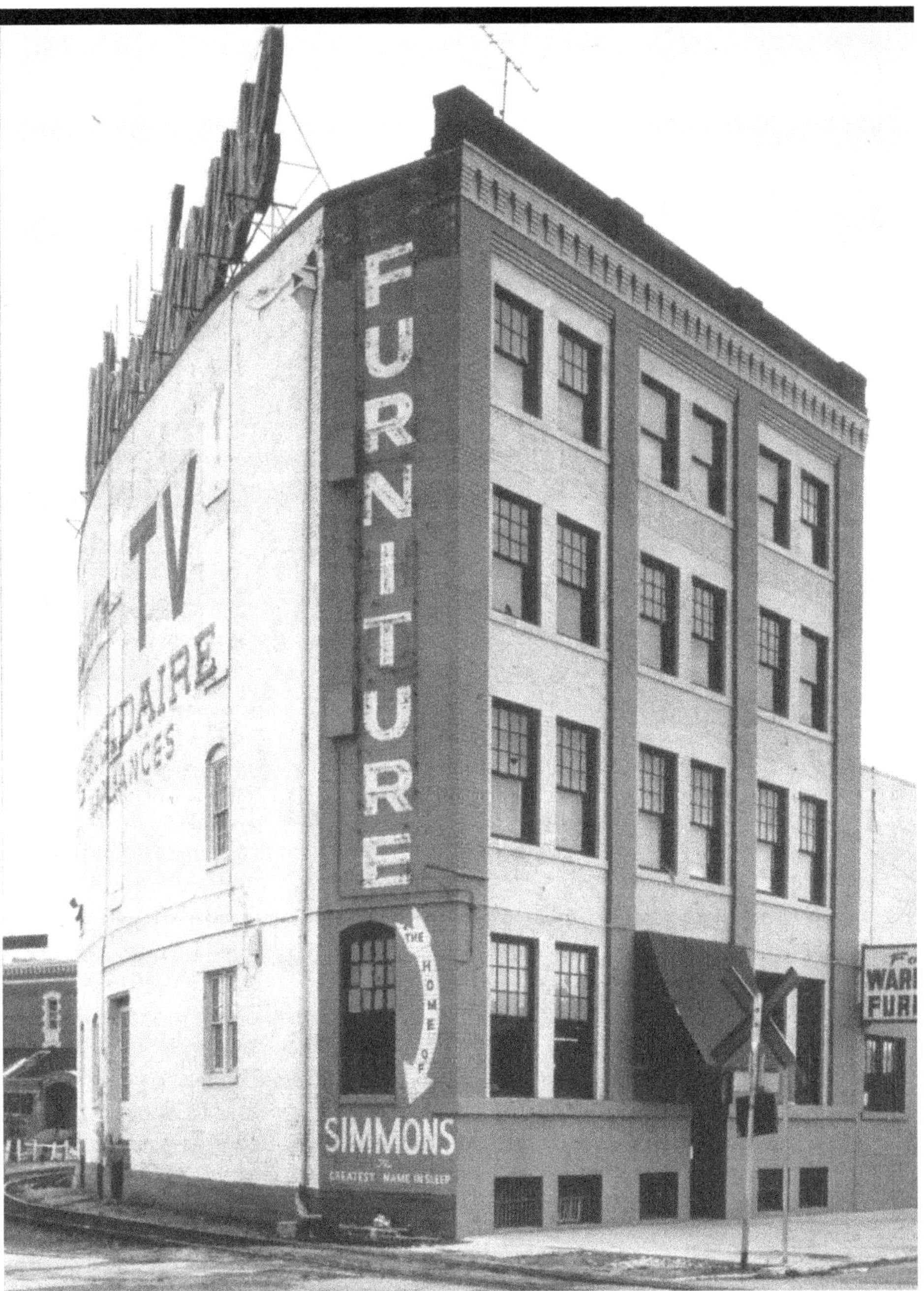

Foster's triangular "flat-iron" warehouse was rounded to accommodate the railroad's downtown right-of-way. The curved north face of the 1910 building has since been encapsulated by a parking garage.

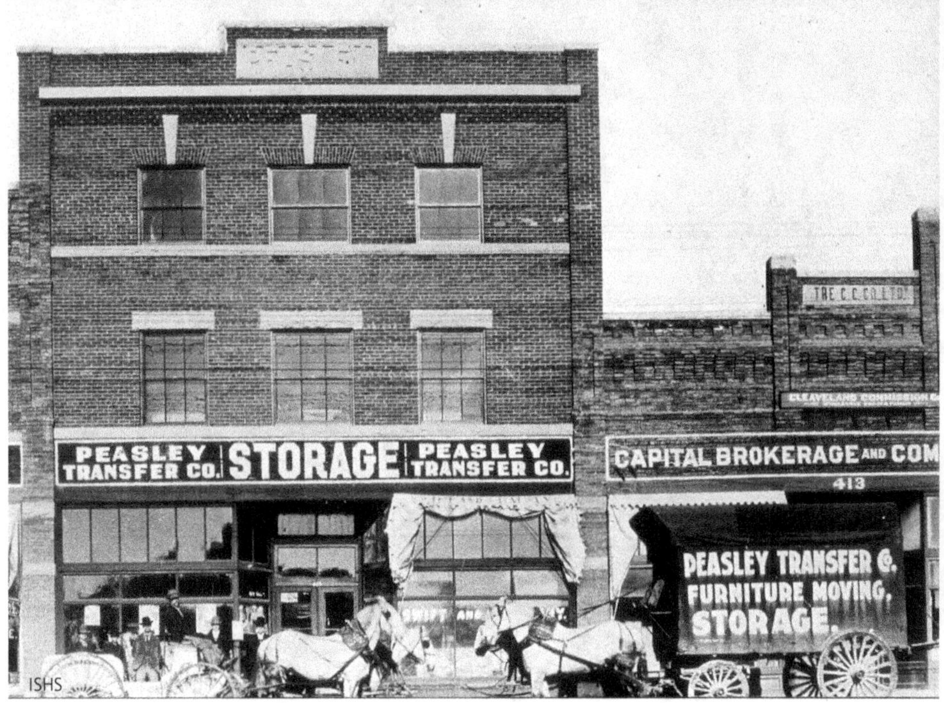

Peasley Transfer Company ran freight from the warehouse district during the heyday of railroad era.

1975, one of the first projects of this type started in the old warehouse district along downtown Boise's 8th Street.

The history of the warehouses reaches back to those far-gone days when the survival of the town depended on the timely arrival of supplies. The city, founded as a trading supply point for miners, needed to expand its ability to store massive amounts of goods awaiting transfer to outlying mining areas. The growth of the city became dependent upon the freighting industry and the warehouses were needed to hold the goods. By the 1870s, the mines in the area started to produce less, but Boise did not follow the fate of many former supply towns by fading away. Instead, it grew as its citizens recognized the potential of the region. The railroads also saw the area's viability and started construction of the Oregon Short Line railway. In 1893, the railroad built a spur line into Boise's downtown area, and soon after came the construction of a fine stone depot and park near 10th and Front streets. Prior to that time orchards owned by Thomas Davis spread along the northern side of the river. Upon receiving word of the railway's intentions to locate downtown, he platted blocks 1, 2 and 3 of the Davis Addition, transforming a section of orchard into a workable spot for a warehouse district. The railroad company's right of way passed through those blocks and in 1902 the first of many new warehouse buildings graced the area. The original set of warehouses stretched between Broad and Myrtle on the west side of 8th Street, with the right-of-way forming an alley behind the buildings. Soon the district expanded in all directions, including another set of buildings between the alley and 9th Street. In 1905-06, a spur line was laid down the center of the alley, bringing the railway cars to the back doors of the buildings.

Boise's prosperity in the early 1900s led to the development of grand buildings—even the warehouses bore stately arches, detailed cornices and stout posts. The warehouse district's wholesalers prospered as they sent goods to Idaho's mining, lumber, agriculture and irrigation industries. The area housed hardware, fruit, grocery and paint wholesalers and serviced industries such as a milling company, an icehouse, a storage company and a creamery. Pulley systems protruded from the sides and backs of many buildings, allowing for the transfer of large crates of merchandise from the red brick warehouses to waiting wagons. Two of Boise's leading architectural firms of the time, Tourtellotte and Hummel and Wayland and Fennell, designed most of the buildings. The front of the warehouses facing the streets usually housed offices and storefronts. Between 1902-1915, a four-block warehouse area featured an array of substantial and beautiful buildings.

The grand age of the railroad came to a halt in the 1940s as roadways carved a path across the nation. Automobiles not only changed the way goods were transported, but also the way Boise grew. Wholesalers moved to areas with newer buildings and easier access to highways and the downtown warehouse district started to decline. By the late 1960s, the construction of the freeway system south of town caused a final exodus from the area, seemingly sealing the fate of the 8th Street warehouse district. The buildings were obsolete for modern day warehousing and the area struggled to find a new identity. In 1975, a development team bought five of the warehouse buildings and hired historic planner John Bertram as project coordinator. Because the buildings were "no longer usable for modern day warehousing," the developers requested that the city change the zoning to commercial use to accommodate a plan for developing an 8th Street Marketplace in the area. In 1977, developers Winston Moore and Larry Leasure started the first phase of the adaptive re-use plan with renovation of the Northrup Hardware and Coffin Building at the corner of Broad and 8th streets. That same year saw the implementation of the North Bank Project, providing a new and historic streetscape on 8th between the bridge and Front Street. In 1978, the South Eighth Street Historic District gained recognition by being placed on the National Register of Historic Places. Then in 1979, renovations came to the buildings on the east side of 8th Street, where shops and office spaces were developed in the Falk, Carlson Lusk Hardware and Boise Elevator buildings. Conversion of the Falk/Davidson garage into a theatre accompanied the 1979 renovations. The only other business on that side of the street, the Idaho Candy Company, had been in existence since 1909, making that Tourtellotte and Hummel building the home of the longest-standing business of the area.

As Boise started to recognize the importance of its historic architecture, preservationists started to recommend areas for local historic districts. In 1982, the city's Historic Preservation Commission made the warehouse district its third official historic district. Ownership of the area changed in 1994 as S-16 Corporation bought the marketplace. The corporation, owned by businessman J.R. Simplot and his grandchildren, expanded the area over the next 10 years, working with the city to develop a cultural district stretching from the 8th Street Bridge to Grove Street. Additional warehouses were renovated in the area to house practice and business space for the ballet, opera, philharmonic and a contemporary theatre. They combined with the area's existing museums and library to create a unique setting in the downtown area. Educators also saw the advantage of being in the district as a private school moved in, again renovating a warehouse building for its use.

In 2003, Brix and Co., a development firm out of Bethesda, MD, bought the 8th Street Marketplace, renaming it Boise Downtown, or BoDo. The new owners released a plan for renovating the market area, calling for new development between Front and Broad streets. One of the structures bought by the BoDo developers was the district's oldest remaining warehouse, the O.W. Smith Building. On the northwest corner of Myrtle and 8th streets, the 1902 two-story structure was built as a warehouse and storefront for Smith and Company, which dealt in essential goods of the day such as seeds, hay, cereals, salt, flour, grain and produce. Otto W. Smith built this store on a site close to the depot's newly developing warehouse district. The fire of 1903 left the Smith Building untouched and it remained the place of business for Smith and Co. until 1908. The front of the building featured a handsome storefront with windows, a canopy and a recessed entryway. The side of the building that faced Myrtle Street housed a series of bays with windows and doors to facilitate the loading of wagons. A system of pulleys and hoists were used to load bags of seed or other products onto wagons parked on the Myrtle side of the building. Most of these features were torn down and replaced with a new wall when the building was renovated. The

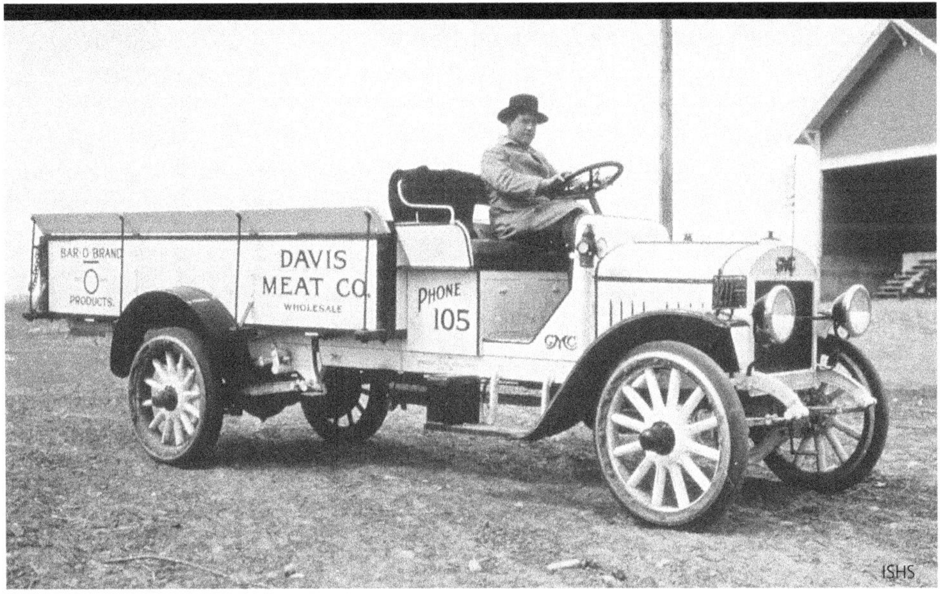

Davis meat truck, 1919. Meat packers had brought cold storage refrigeration to the warehouse district by 1910.

original architectural features provided a visual reminder of Boise's history, illustrating the working history of mule packers and pack trains and the vitally important service they provided to the people of the area as well as the early economy of the city. While the storefront had received structural updates, the previous owners had done little to improve the warehouse portion of the building. It had substandard electrical wiring, no modern heat and many other things that were needed to make the space easily adaptable for modern business use. Over time many of the front and side windows had been altered and the recessed entryway had been filled in and made flush with the front of the building. The brick had been painted and a side rail of cheap concrete had been added to the Myrtle Street side when the Connector was built.

Instead of renovating the building as their 2003 plan indicated, the BoDo team sold the building in 2005 to local developer Gary Christensen, who submitted a plan that same year to the Planning and Zoning Department to completely demolish the building, citing costly procedures to renovate the structure. Christensen proposed tearing the structure down and reconstructing a commercial and residential building that would "keep the character" of the area. Because of the building's location in a historic district, the plans needed the approval of the Historic Preservation Commission, which ruled against a complete demolition of the building. In October of 2005, the eight-person commission heard a second proposal by Christensen, which focused on keeping only the front wall of the storefront on 8th Street. The plan called for the demolition of all but 10 percent of the original structure and construction of a new building behind the old façade. Developers would then add a third story to the new building that would be set back from the original storefront. The new design also incorporated the next-door Peasley Building into the plan. Historic planner Bertram and historic architect Dan Everhart both wanted more from the developer. Everhart argued that the real historic value of the building lay in its Myrtle Street wall, whose architecture displayed one of the last visual images of the days the freight wagons. He also reminded the group that demolishing 90 percent of a building is not now, nor ever will be, considered a historic preservation technique. The developers objected to keeping the Myrtle Street wall because of a masonry shear test showing deterioration of the brick on that side of the building. They argued that the cost of renovating the wall would be prohibitive.

The Historic Commission focused on two criteria in determining the fate of the building: whether the changes adversely affected the nature of the Historic District and whether historic renovation proved economically feasible for the owner. In the commission's opinion, the commercial storefront of the building represented the primary façade of historic significance and by keeping that, the plan did not adversely affect the nature of the district. They noted the preservation of many architectural features on the front façade as essential to keeping the historical accuracy of the building. In Everhart's opinion, the Myrtle Street façade represented the only readable face defining the building as a warehouse and that losing it did indeed subtract from the "historic fabric" of the district. The commission's second issue of interest centered on the economic feasibility of renovating the original structure. They concluded that the cost to bring the building up to the seismic standards required by building codes created a financial hardship for the owner and that in the opinion of the staff it would be impossible to restore the deteriorating brick in an aesthetically pleasing manner. Thus, renovation would not be economically feasible for the owner. One commissioner, while supporting the project, also brought up the concern that "peeling away" so much of the building may not only be stripping away at the warehouse's his-

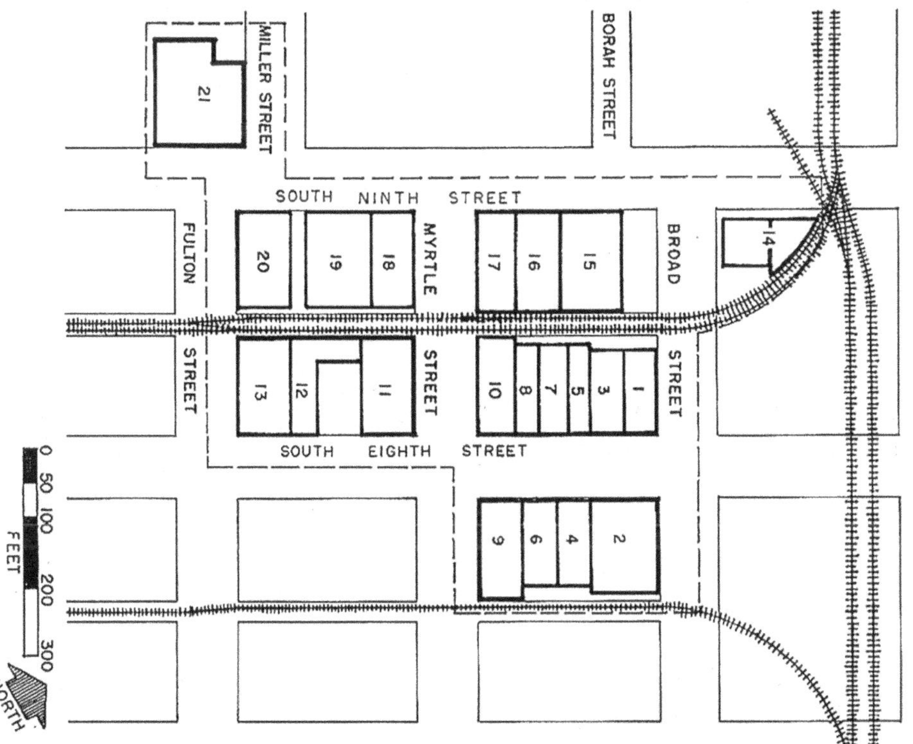

The success of San Francisco's Ghiradelli Square inspired warehouse renovation on Boise's South Eighth Street. Pictured: map of the proposed Eighth Street warehouse district, 1979.

tory but may jeopardize the structure's National Registry status. Bertram later voiced this same concern about the district as a whole. He noted that many small changes had been made to the buildings since their placement on the National Register of Historic Places. Those changes, added to the loss of the oldest building in the district, could place the designation at risk, he suggested.

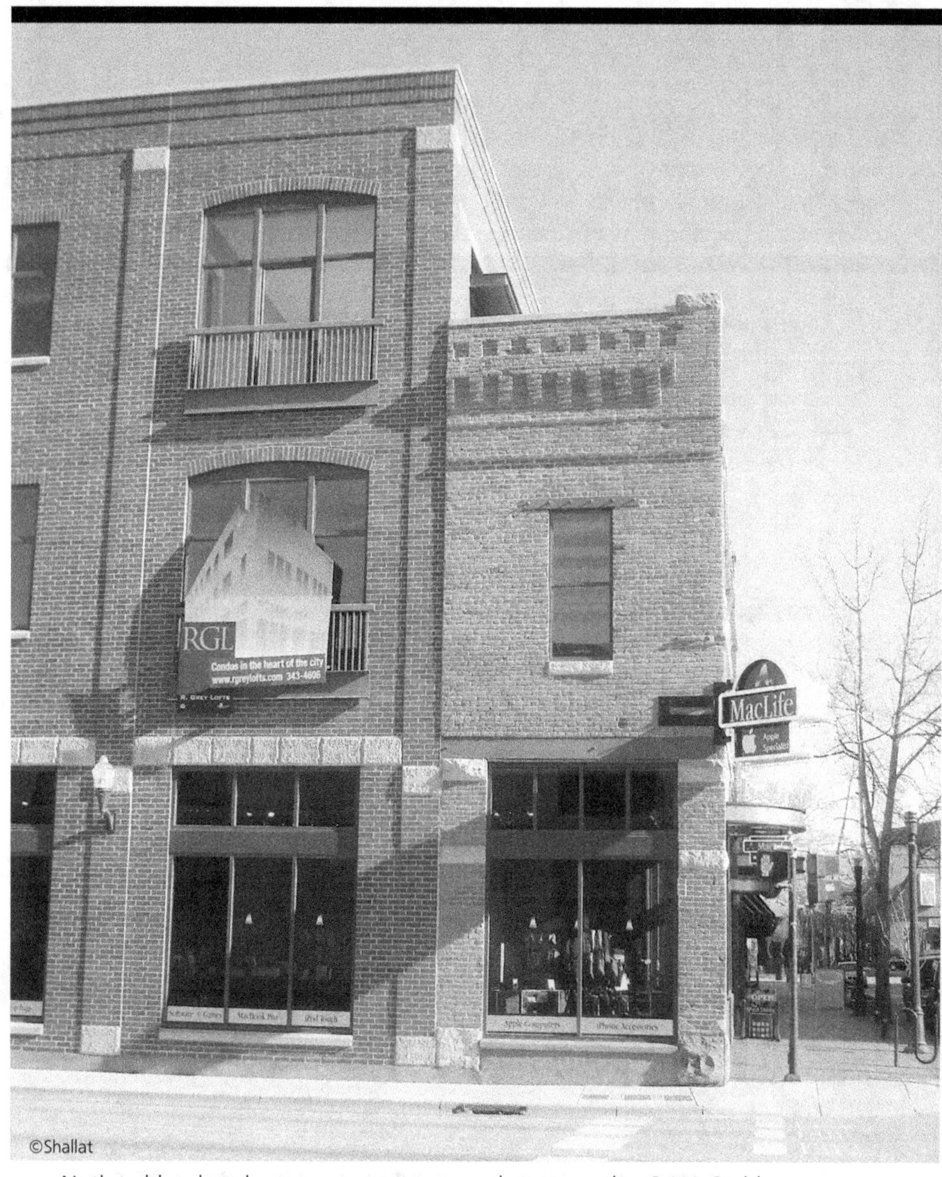

©Shallat

National landmark status was not enough to save the O.W. Smith warehouse. Only the facade (center of photo) remains from the original building, which was torn down in 2006.

At the October 2005 meeting it became apparent that Historic Register status was not driving the decision. It was, as one member commented, economics. The usability of the building became the bottom line, and the adverse affect of possibly having the building remain empty seemed of more importance than keeping the historic fabric in place. In the end the commission ruled in favor of the developer's second plan, with the condition that the original storefront be retained as presented by Bertram in three historic photos of the building. The 2005 decision on the O.W. Smith Building marked a change in focus on the part of the Historic Preservation Commission. In this case, promoting the city's economic welfare became more central to the discussion than promoting its cultural and educational welfare. While commissioners talked about architectural aspects of the building and "retaining the character" of the area, little was voiced about preserving the actual history of the district. Historic fabric goes beyond design elements such as beams, cornices and pilasters. It includes a discussion of the working history of the area and the contributions the people who worked in the warehouses made to the city. That history speaks, maybe ironically, about the city's economic past and its earliest means of economic stability. Rather than consider the warehouse's role in Boise's working history, the commission focused on how to reoccupy the building.

While the city should be concerned with preserving only historically appropriate buildings, it seems an unnecessary battle in historic districts where their significance has already been established. It is also undisputable that the economic viability of Boise's downtown core is of vital importance, but one has to question any precedent set by the Historic Preservation Commission to trade that for historical integrity when working within historic districts. While much of the O.W. Smith Building may have met the criteria for demolition due to the high cost of renovation and saving the façade at least brings coherency to the streetscape, the designation of the front as the primary façade of historical significance was simply not justified by the history of the district. A project that focuses on preserving only the front 10 percent of the building, while destroying the wall that truly speaks to the historic nature of the district, cannot truly be called historic preservation of the building. After all what is historic preservation without the history?

• • •

Ann Felton graduated from Boise State with a BBA in accountancy in 1981 and a master's degree in history in 2007. She is an adjunct professor in the history department.

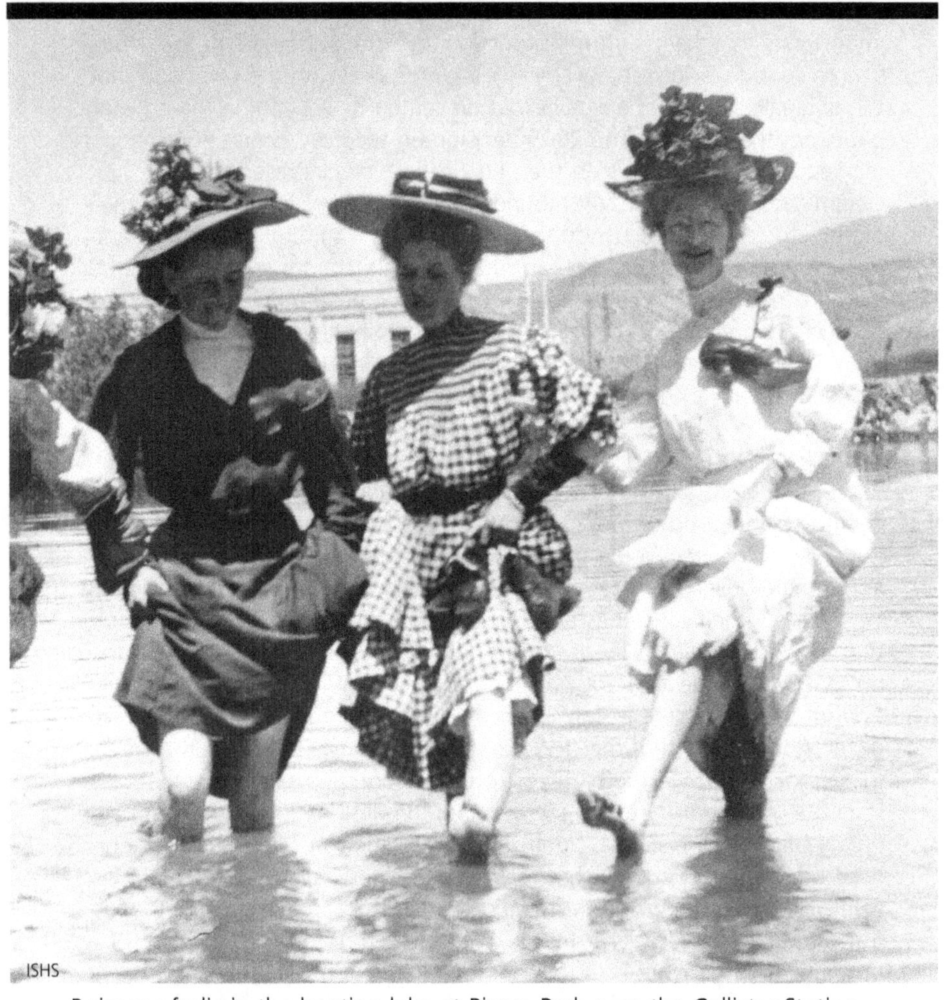

Boiseans frolic in the boating lake at Pierce Park near the Collister Station, about 1908.

Creating
COLLISTER
by William Blackadar

Nestled against the northwest Boise foothills, the greater Collister area was once a distant trolley stop in an agriculturally centered community three miles away from the hustle of Boise City. Today, it's a place with deep community roots, stemming from early generosity and maturing into the neighborhood that residents have molded into a community. Bordered by State Street on its southwestern edge, Pierce Park Lane to the west, Cartwright and Hill roads to the north, and Taft and 36th streets to the south and east, the Collister area exists comfortably between the downtown economic center and the residential expansions toward Eagle. But due to its location, the Collister area, like many Boise neighborhoods, faces the challenges of urban sprawl.

The Collister neighborhood derives its name posthumously after Dr. George Collister, called a "pioneer" in his Oct. 19, 1935, obituary in *The Idaho Daily Statesman*. Upon graduating in 1880 from Heron Medical

College in Cleveland, Dr. Collister was convinced by his sister Julia, who already lived in Idaho, to leave his native Ohio and move west. Being the wife of Idaho Supreme Court Judge Joseph Huston, apparently his sister was a persuasive woman. Dr. Collister and his wife Mary Elizabeth moved to Boise, where he opened a downtown office on Main Street in June of 1881. Advertising as a specialist in pediatrics, Dr. Collister was one of the first to bring public health services to the Treasure Valley. He served twice on the city council, where he was instrumental in creating numerous health and sanitation ordinances. He served as city and county physician and was physician at the Idaho State Penitentiary and at the Soldier's Home, according to his obituary.

An avid writer and horticulturalist, Dr. Collister became the owner of one of the valley's first peach orchards. Shaded by nearly 11,000 peach, prune and various other fruit trees, Dr. Collister built a 20-bedroom mansion overlooking the developing orchard on some 245 acres owned by him and his sister a few miles west of the city limits on Valley Road, now State Street. Though many of the orchard's original trees have since died or been cut down, numerous others still bear fruit to this day. Collister's mansion, built by the noted architectural firm Tourtellotte and Hummel near the junction of present-day Sycamore and Taft streets, was converted into the Elks Rehab Medical Care Center after Dr. Collister's death. The house has since been torn down and Boise City Fire Station No.9 now occupies the original home site. Of the 245 acres that Dr. Collister owned, about 150 acres were donated for a new school site, leaving ample open space for children to play. First opened to students in the fall of 1911, Collister Elementary on Catalpa Drive is currently Boise's smallest elementary school, serving 185 students from the Collister neighborhood. The remaining acreage was subsequently sold to R.H. and Elton Davidson, who subdivided the newly acquired land in 1944, forming the heart of what is now called the Sycamore neighborhood, nestled between Taft and Sycamore streets and Catalpa Drive to the north. The Sycamore neighborhood is unique because of its 101 acres of similarly designed and oriented lots; the acreage was divided into 98 7/8-acre parcels that allowed one horse, one cow and 150 chickens on each, believing that lots could be self-supporting with room for a large garden. To this day, special covenants make it the only neighborhood in Boise that still formally allows agricultural stock on each lot.

Officially existing outside of the Boise city limits until the mid-1970s, the Collister neighborhood was tethered to the bustling city by rail at the dawn of the 20th century. The Boise Interurban Railway Company constructed a main stop and shelter at the intersection with Valley Road and Collister, wrote historian Arthur Hart in the Jan. 9, 2007 *Idaho Statesman*. Terry's State Street Saloon currently occupies the site of the old Collister Station-Boise Interurban stop. With the completion of the Collister Mercantile Company in 1910 at the same intersection, the Collister area had the begin-

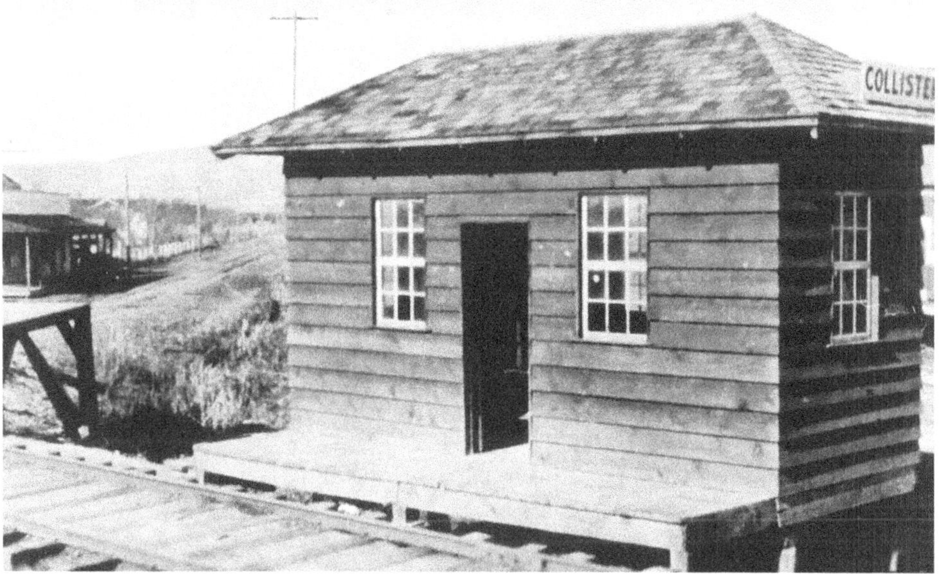

Collister Depot on Valley Road, about 1910. Today the site of the boardwalk depot is occupied by Terry's State Street Saloon.

nings of a small, quiet, agricultural community. Mixed use in nature, the wood-framed building operated as a grocery and general store through the 1940s.

Some historians believe that State Street's width can be attributed to the streetcar. Rather than building new tracks or roads over already-existing rail bed, it was not uncommon for planners and engineers to synergistically incorporate rails alongside or within roads. Now all but a memory, Boise's bustling trolley system has had ripple effects through time. Without the advent of the trolley at the beginning of the 20th century, the Treasure Valley would arguably look much different than it does today. With investments in and along the trolley line, many distinct neighborhoods in the country became notable destinations, including the Natatorium, the city of Caldwell, and Pierce and Curtis parks in Boise. The planners of the new Boise

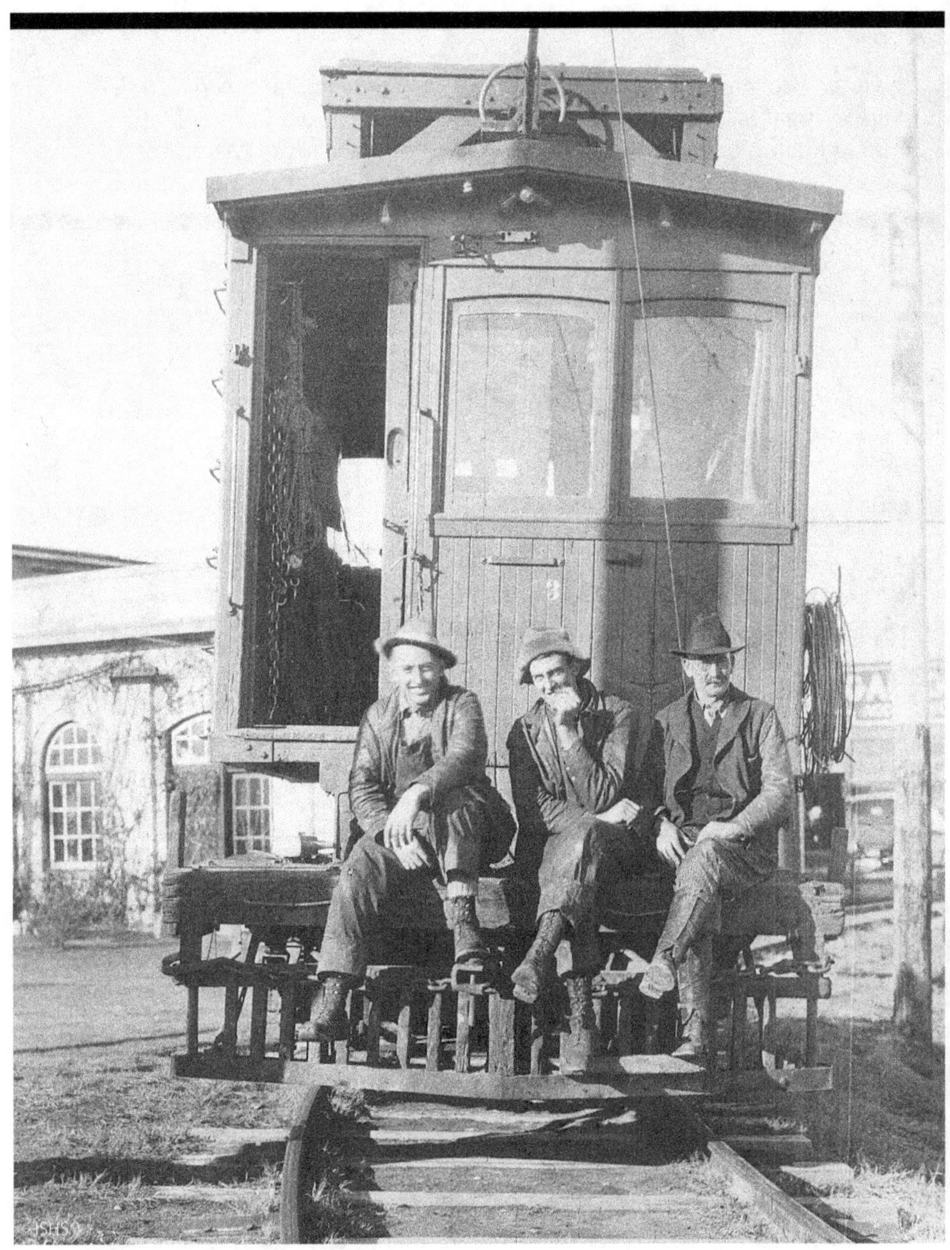

Walter Pierce's interurban railroad linked Collister to Caldwell via Middleton. Pictured: Car No. 99 at the Middleton substation, about 1920.

and Interurban line realized from the beginning that the electric trolley cars could generate extra revenue if they created special destinations for pleasure seekers. School kids on field trips, church groups and families on Sunday outings began riding the cars for picnics, holidays or birthday parties ... or just to see the sights along the way. One could ride the rails from downtown Boise to Collister Station for a mere 5 cents.

Walter E. Pierce, a successful entrepreneur from Kansas, promoted one of the first "destinations" along the trolley line. Being the sole real estate broker in the new North End and Resseguie developments closer to the city, Pierce turned his attention further north along the rail line that he had invested in, which sparked the development of what is now known as Pierce Park. With the new Interurban running down State Street (Valley Road) and throughout the valley, remote land in the country became accessible. In a matter of a few years,

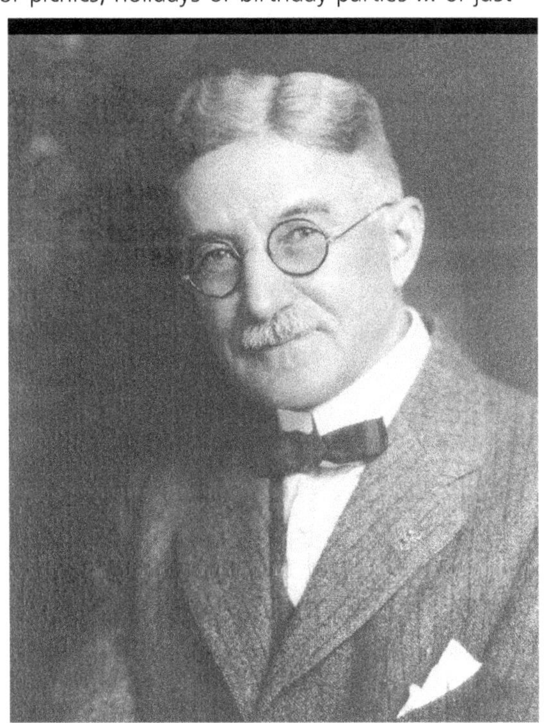

Real estate tycoon Walter E. Pierce pioneered the Boise-to-Caldwell interurban railroad. In 1908, he opened Pierce Park.

Pierce Park provided a grand recreation spot for the modern electric world when it opened in 1908. A mere three miles from Collister Station, the park featured an electric-lighted entrance archway, picnic areas, a baseball diamond and a dance pavilion, among other things.

But today's Collister is far different than the idyllic community that thrived 100 years ago. Cities are an evolving collection of communities built by people to serve their vision of well-being. Dr. Collister originally envisioned a rural lifestyle near Boise where he could enjoy his orchards and be close to the cultural and economic hub of the valley. The development of the

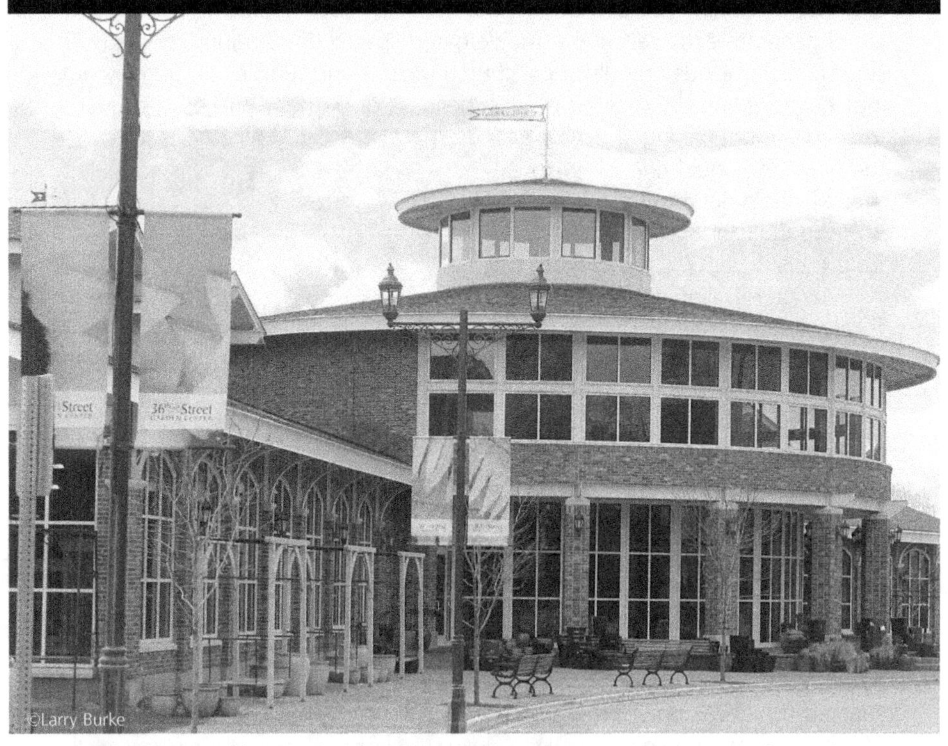

A neighborhood in renaissance: The 36th Street Garden Center, above, is a recent addition to the commercial life of Collister. In 2008 the City of Boise also opened its first neighborhood branch library in the Collister Shopping Center.

Interurban streetcar line made the area more accessible, prompting the creation of one of the valley's early suburbs. Today we see a similar pattern—people want a bit of country near an urban area. Then as transportation corridors are built to serve these first groups, more people follow, filling the open space that they sought to enjoy. First it was Collister, then Eagle. Now Star and points west are seeing this evolution. Thus, Collister has gone through a decline as people saw the area as neither rural nor suburban nor urban. Some observers say it is a community that has lost its sense of place, lost its sense of identity. Rurally and socially intertwined with the bustling economic centers of downtown, the 'New North End' and the now more tony subdivisions toward Eagle, the Collister neighborhood may be straddling the line between possible blight and continued development.

Threatened by infill, sprawl, crime, noise and suffocating traffic, to name a few, residents, as well as the rest of the city, are taking steps to change the neighborhood for the better. Through a combination of coordinated efforts by its residents and Boise City initiatives, Collister is now an example of a neighborhood in renaissance. Today, the area is seeing revitalization that started with a few committed residents. The Collister Association has developed a neighborhood plan that has become a part of Boise City's Comprehensive Plan. The association has advocated before the Ada County Highway District to improve the major State Street arterial and eventually construct a roundabout at 36th Street. The roundabout will be the final infrastructure improvement in what is becoming a small commercial node that includes the local junior high school and the redevelopment of the old nursery renamed as the 36th Street Garden Center that now includes retail, restaurant and work-live space. As a result, it is projected that over the next 20 years, households in this area could grow by 7 percent and jobs in the area could increase by 25 percent. This urbanization is supported and encouraged by the city through neighborhood grants to improve local infrastructure such as sidewalks and direct investment with the 2008 opening of Boise's first neighborhood library in the refurbished Collister Shopping Center. In the first six months more than 70,000 individual visits were made to the new branch library, and the library loans about 16,000 items every month. The future is bright for the area, with plans to create a high-speed bus rapid transit system on State Street, thus giving residents an alternative to the auto and relieving commuter pressure on the local roads. The construction of a roundabout will increase the pedestrian access between the junior high and nearby businesses and homes. New townhouse developments, new commercial ventures and a renaissance of neighborhood services blend with Collister's unique character, where residential rural lots nestle among new and old subdivisions, where roosters can be heard in the morning and cattle graze on a summer evening.

• • •

William Blackadar will graduate from Boise State in May with a BA in environmental studies. He resides in Salmon, where he guides whitewater trips and works on his family's ranch. He may attend law school in the future and will continue running wild rivers throughout the world.

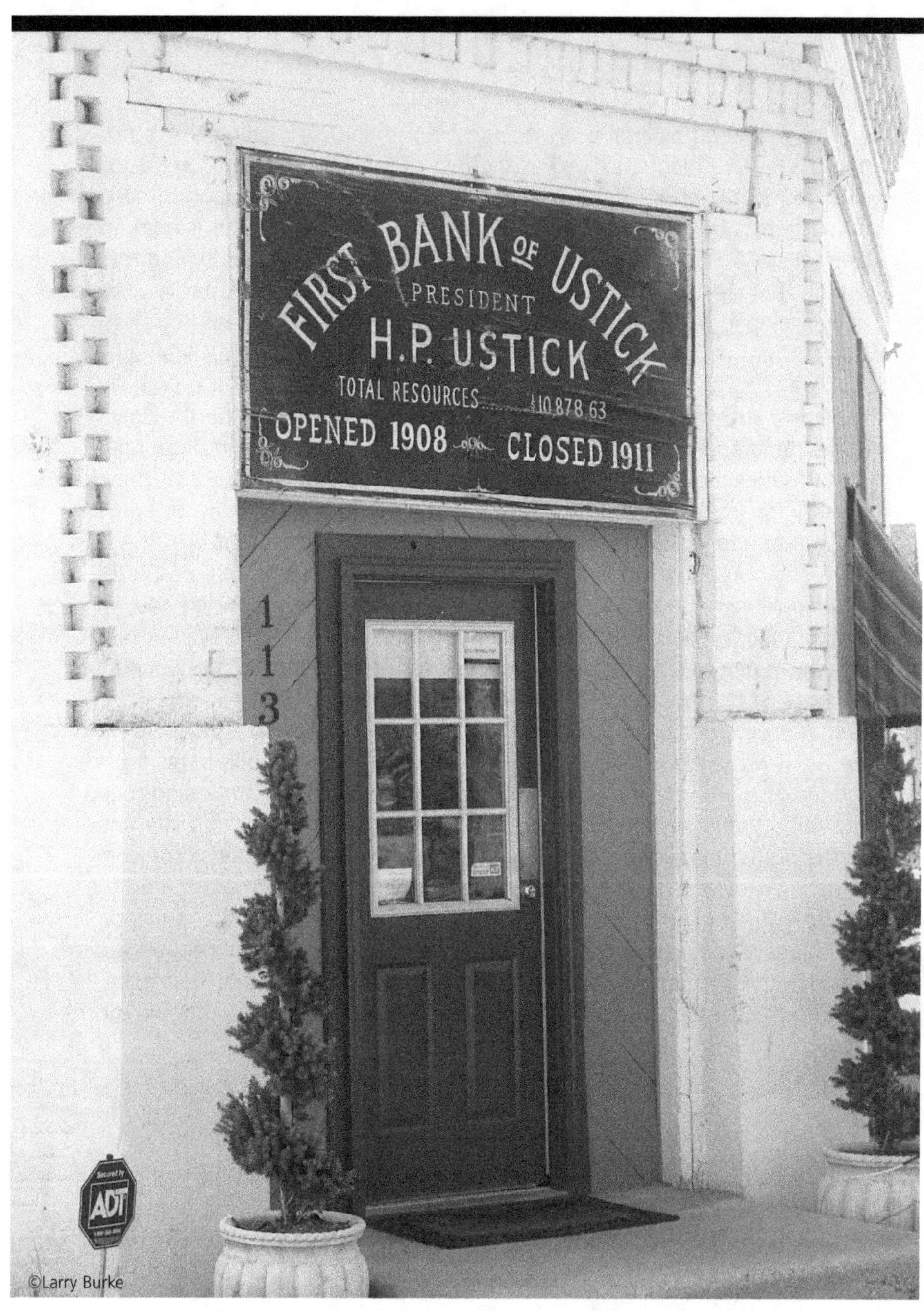

©Larry Burke

Dentist Harlan P. Ustick platted his streetcar township in 1907. Pictured: the 1908 First Bank of Ustick, a survivor from the trolley era.

Ustick on the brink of PLACE

by Ted Venegas

The Ustick townsite once had acres of orchards, an effective public transportation system and a largely self-contained community environment. Over time, the automobile replaced the Interurban rail system and suburban development in Boise methodically devoured the orchards that once characterized the area. Consequently, the neighborhood lost the sense of place it once held, and so lost its community and historic identity. Long-time resident Gladys Clymens recalled when Ustick was still considered a place. "Even as a child living in the townsite during the 1940s and 1950s, I thought of Ustick as my home town. It had not yet become a suburb of Boise." Alarmed by the continued erosion of their community and lack of input on development decisions, neighborhood leaders organized into one of Boise's most effective neighborhood associations. They have since made strides in determining their own future and have taken on issues such as infill development, historic preservation and, more recently, the controversial Ustick road-widening project. However, Ustick continues to teeter on the brink of place. Local policy decisions will ultimately determine if this historic

Boise community will regain its former identity or continue to fall into fragmentation.

Prior to World War II, agricultural communities like Ustick were common across the country. Farmers and ranchers brought produce to these centers to be shipped and sold. Their families attended the churches and schools and shopped at the markets. Beyond this, these townsites served as places where rural people met each other, communed and discussed the issues of the day. In modern urbanist terminology, they existed as "place," familiar and vibrant to those who lived, worked and socialized within their boundaries. Many of these areas lost their sense of place as transportation and development policies resulted in the conversion of villages into suburban strip malls and parking lots. Where public transportation once centralized communities, automobile-centered planning has fragmented them. In *How Cities Work*, Alex Marshall metaphorically describes this phenomenon in comparing pre-World War II communities to modern ones: "Newer places have no fabric at all. It's the difference between a well-knit sweater and a pile of yarn." The old Ustick townsite fits Marshall's metaphor well. Though it is an older neighborhood, the loss of the Interurban railway, low interest in the area's history and the lack of growth management turned what was once a well-knit sweater into an indiscernible pile of yarn.

One of the most important threads knitting Ustick together was its Interurban rail system. While apple orchards formed the economic base for the farming communities in the west valley, public and product transportation built the foundation for townsites. The streetcar system spurred development of the areas around Boise and helped make suburban growth popular. By the turn of the century rail had been laid throughout the valley, connecting remote farming communities such Eagle, Star and Middleton. In 1907, the Boise Valley Railroad Company completed the streetcar lines running west from Boise to Fairview Hill and Ustick. Ustick Road later had rail tracks running along its full length connecting Caldwell to Boise. The Interurban, as the popular rail system came to be known, was completed by 1912 and allowed farmers to ship their produce easily from outlying areas into the commercial hub of Boise. Just as important, it allowed rural residents to commute in an affordable and timely manner, socially and economically connecting these small, remote communities to each other. Early schedules show that a person could hop the trolley in Ustick and be to Boise within 20 minutes. Today's automobile commuters would be hard pressed to match that time on the congested roadways.

The rail company ownership roster listed some of Boise's founding families, including Lemp, Ustick, Sonna, Pierce and Noble, who as stakeholders in the valley had ample incentive to see it prosper. In the long run the enterprise did not prove to be solvent, as expenses were extremely high and profitable years were few and far between. By the 1930s, the automobile had replaced rail as the dominant form of personal transportation, effectively

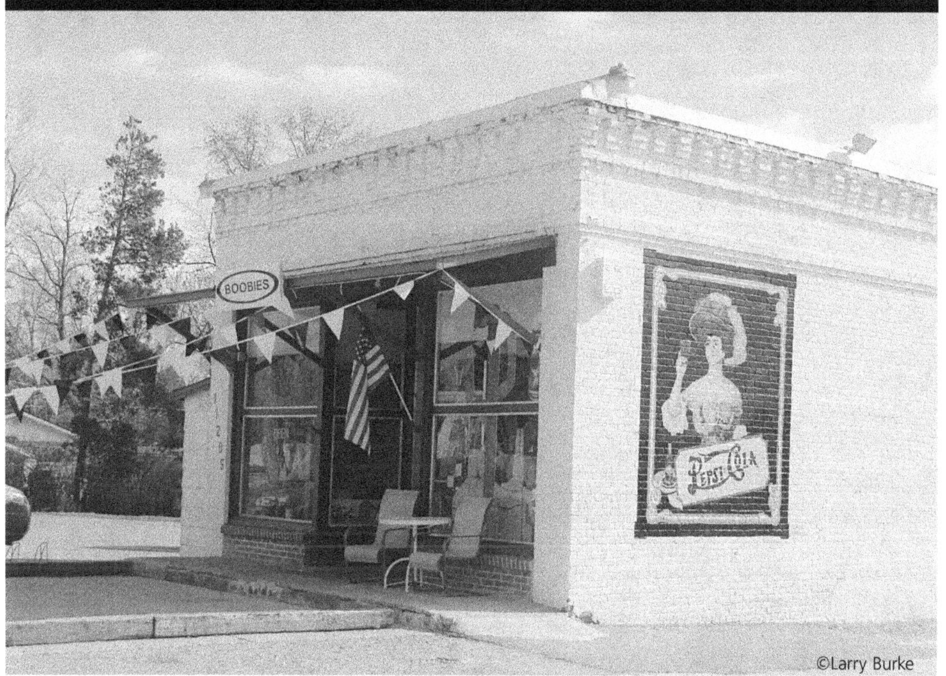

A Victorian lady advertises cola on Ustick Road. The store opened in 1912.

sounding the death knell for many rail systems throughout the western United States. The Interurban managed to hang on until 1928, when its heyday as an initiator and connector of communities ended.

One of the Interurban's biggest supporters was dentist Harlan P. Ustick. Though he was one of Boise's pioneers and founders, little information on him is available. What does exist ties him to various business ventures in the valley. Dr. Ustick moved from Ohio in 1903 to the agricultural settlement between Boise and Meridian, where he purchased a ranch-style house and ran the third-largest apple orchard in the valley. It was under his influence that the Interurban was routed along Market Street in 1907, later renamed Ustick Road, and along the land that he had newly acquired and platted. The initial 110 plots that he purchased came to form the original Ustick townsite. A 1907 *Idaho Statesman* article exclaimed that, "Ustick would soon be a live bustling village ... although little effort has been made to sell the lots, 28 have already been sold." Today there are few remnants of

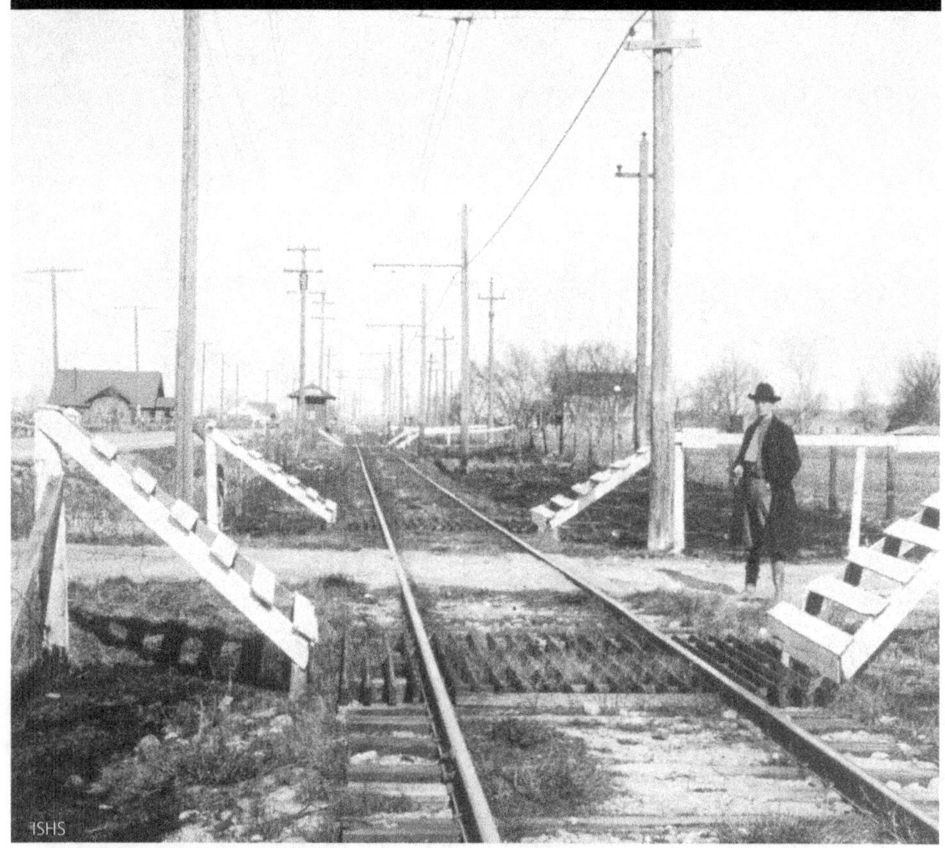

Cattle guards at a West Boise trolley crossing. Streetcars linked Boise to Ustick in 1907.

the village that bears Dr. Ustick's name. The store, the bank and the school are the only public buildings that have survived time and progress, and each has undergone a number of incarnations over the years. Period residential homes still dot the neighborhood, including Dr. Ustick's original home, but even these are becoming rare as developers scurry to acquire valuable land.

Despite its history and the fact that many pre-World War II residents still call Ustick home, the neighborhood continues to spiral into a blighted state. Residential and commercial development projects not fitting with the existing form have altered the character of Ustick so much that its historic identity is hardly recognizable. During the 1990s a number of concerned Ustick residents banded together in an effort to promote a historic district designation for the old townsite, hoping to preserve what little remained. The movement for this type of designation among Ustick residents intensified and blossomed, especially as development and infill projects loomed over their neighborhoods.

As part of the West Valley Neighborhood Association, the community came together to put a voice to Ustick's legacy and future. The city of Boise was receptive to the idea of historic districts to combat the rapid growth and urban sprawl that were consuming farmland and open space at an alarming rate. With as much, if not more, history than other historic districts, Ustick residents were confident that they had something significant to offer. Tricia Canaday, the Boise historic preservation planner at the time, commented that with historic district status Ustick residents would "gain the reassurance that their historic fabric will be maintained and preserved." This became increasingly important to Ustick residents who had witnessed a pattern of strip malls, big box stores and cookie-cutter houses becoming more prominent throughout the region. The neighborhood had begun to understand that in order to restore and preserve place, while staving off undesired development, they would need to organize and put together a vision.

In anticipation of historic district designation, community leaders and activists in 1997 collaborated to form a united vision for the area and pressed the city for action. Ultimately they looked to Hyde Park and Harrison Boulevard in Boise's North End as examples of what they would like to see for Ustick. Hyde Park, once a neighborhood commercial center, had become a destination point for visitors who enjoyed the history, architecture and quaintness of the area. But consensus among residents and the city deteriorated into philosophical and economic disagreements. The concept of historic preservation collided with Idaho's deeply-rooted tradition of property rights. Idaho is a state built on the western tradition of individual and property rights, and more often than not this mentality encourages policy that trumps the common good. Though most Idahoans might agree on the importance of historical heritage and preservation, they likely would not agree that this should interfere with the rights of people to do as they wish with their property. With these obstacles to overcome, the vision for a historic district in the old Ustick townsite dissolved as quickly as it had evolved, and the area's identity continued to teeter on the brink of extinction.

Though the opportunity for a historic district appeared lost, the hope for a rebirth of the Ustick townsite still lingered in the minds of many neighborhood residents. Some community leaders looked for ideas that might settle the central differences that continued to divide the neighborhood. By the late 1990s, concepts such as Smart Growth and New Urbanism became common vernacular in planning and urban studies circles. These ideas stressed a return to an era when architecture resonated with a sense of place, communities were pedestrian-friendly, and public transit was both accessible and affordable. Their philosophies were the antithesis to the sprawling suburbs that sucked life out of the towns and cities and made humanity more dependent on the introverted and soulless automobile.

In *Suburban Nation* Andres Duany states that Americans have been "building a national landscape that is largely devoid of places worth caring about." Our American heritage has embedded us with the idea that it is our God-given right to have our plot of land, tall fences and complete privacy from the outside world. Unfortunately, this has alienated us from the community, and indeed Americans are in the process of desensitizing themselves to the need for community. Reversing this negative trend has become the goal of planners, architects and environmentalists, as well as that segment of the public concerned with problems associated with rampant, unregulated development.

In the spirit of this New Urbanism ideal, a team of students and researchers from the University of Idaho's Urban Research and Design Center (IURDC) in Boise approached the West Valley Neighborhood Association (WVNA). The design team was initially presented with a number of local neighborhoods to choose from, including historic areas of Vista, Pierce Park and Ustick. They chose the Ustick townsite neighborhood because it presented an opportunity to work with an area that had a history of community as well as an organized and motivated neighborhood association. The team proceeded with a grant from the Treasure Valley Futures Project, a non-profit organization that studies the links between transportation and land use. The WVNA was specifically interested in this project because it provided an opportunity to reinvent the neighborhood without the challenges associated with a historic district. The IURDC plan emphasized the importance of designing around the historic identity of the old Ustick townsite, keeping in mind both the integrity of the older structures and the traditional agricultural identity.

In 1999, just months after the IURDC project was completed, the neighborhood association solicited the Boise State University Department of Public Policy and Administration to conduct a neighborhood survey, the results of which contributed to the final draft of the neighborhood plan. The goal of the survey was to get an idea of how the Ustick residents viewed their neighborhood and what kind of future development patterns they would like to see. Results indicated that the neighborhood's vision conformed to each of the models created by the IURDC design team: citizens valued a pedestrian-friendly community, an environment conducive to human interaction and a neighborhood atmosphere that acknowledged its historic identity. Clearly, the residents desired a neighborhood model that resembled, or at least paid tribute to, the way Ustick was before the Interurban gave way to the automobile and the farms to urban sprawl. They also wanted a traditional marketplace that recreated the social and communal impressions that the Ustick village once had. The overriding theme was the townsite residents' yearning for place in its most genuine context of familiarity and community.

The final version of the neighborhood plan, completed in 2001, focused on five central components: land use, community design, transportation, parks, recreation and cultural resources, and economic development. Each component encouraged neighborhood interaction, which is critical in reclaiming place and identity in the community. Progress on the five planning components has been slow, however. A grant for funds to write a preservation ordinance that would give residents some control over future development was not approved. The Ustick neighborhood plan was adopted by the City of Boise, which made it a part of the city's comprehensive plan. But until language from the plan is implemented as ordinances or codes, Ustick will continue as it has, with few safeguards placed on the history and integrity of the area.

One of the most pressing issues in Ustick revolves around transportation corridors and their future expansion. In 2006, a plan by the Ada County Highway District (ACHD) to widen Ustick Road to five lanes was met with local criticism and led to a jurisdictional dispute, with the ACHD claiming control over city roads and the City of Boise claiming control over land use issues, including the protection of neighborhood integrity. After a long debate and an eventual lawsuit, the ACHD won in court and Ustick was widened to five lanes, without the neighborhood's suggestions for separated sidewalks and landscaped medians to promote pedestrian activity and calm traffic flows. Though the old townsite neighborhood was not immediately impacted by the project, neighbors have been told that future widening will

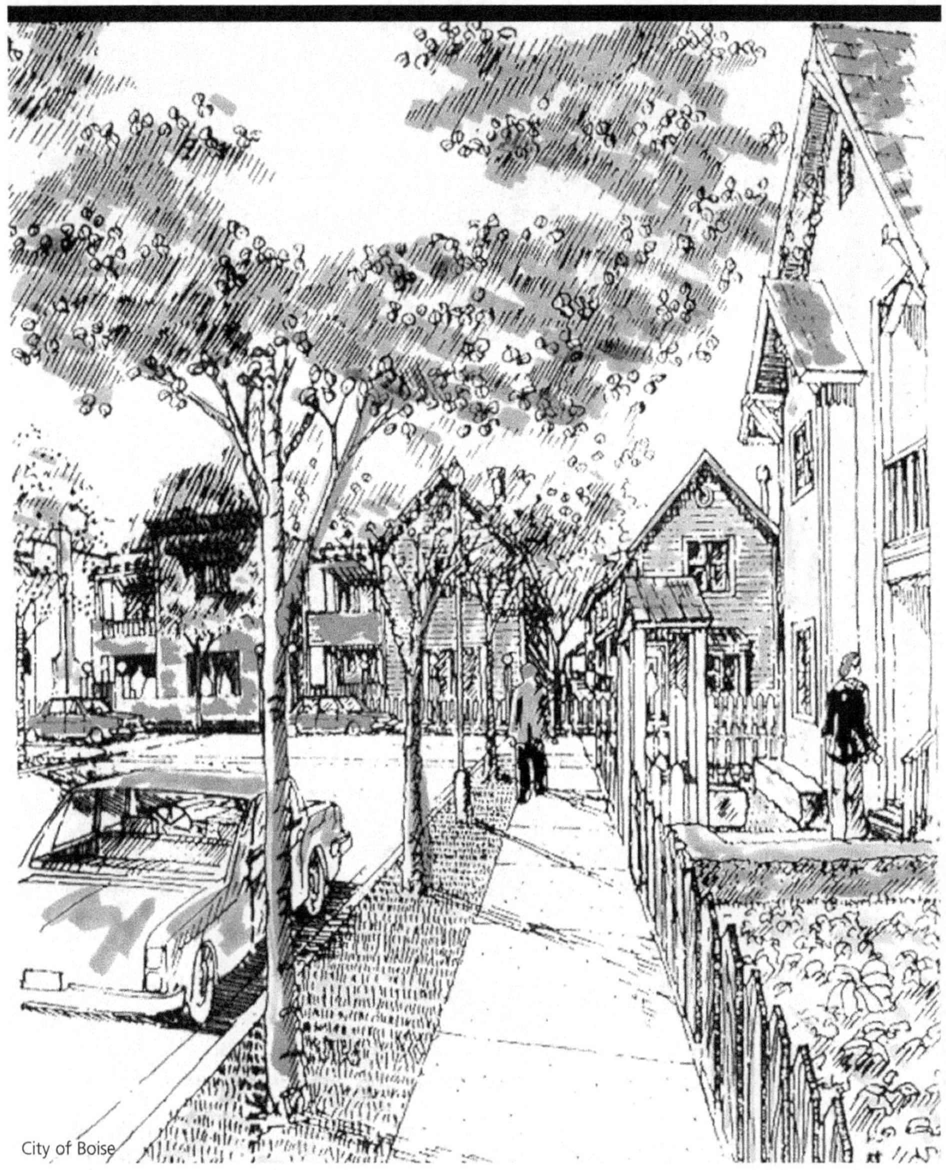

City of Boise

Boise's 1997 master plan proposed walkable streets, corner stores and bus stops for Ustick from Mitchell Street to Maple Grove.

eventually extend into their area. This spurred them to take a proactive approach, and to gain better leverage they are working with other neighborhood associations along Ustick. Resigned to the idea that widening will occur, the WVNA provided a proposal of its own to ACHD for any projects impacting the old townsite. The plan includes the classic boulevard-style expansion with landscaped medians and turn lanes, detached sidewalks, bike lanes and large-growth trees framing each side of the road.

Most Boiseans, unaware of the rich history of the Ustick townsite, tend to have little concern for its future. Development decisions that threaten the neighborhood's integrity might go uncontested or even meet with approval from outsiders who only want their morning commute to go more smoothly. One way to combat this mentality is through historic and cultural education. Neighborhood leaders would like to see some sort of historic recognition for the area in the form of a centennial celebration or historic entry signs. But a lack of funding has resulted in the status quo. Decision makers must understand their roles in determining how our communities will evolve. When we allow markets to dictate growth with little or ineffective regulation, the result is disconnected communities and inefficient transportation systems. We also tend to lose pieces of our past because in the commercial world, history is not seen as economically valuable. It is past time for local governments to come up with a creative solution that reevaluates the paradigm of land-use and infrastructure planning. A more holistic approach that takes into account social concerns as well as the environment and property rights is the only way to a sustainable future.

• • •

Ted Vanegas graduated from Boise State in 2006 with a master's degree in urban/environmental history. He has worked as a city planner for the City of Eagle and teaches at the College of Western Idaho.

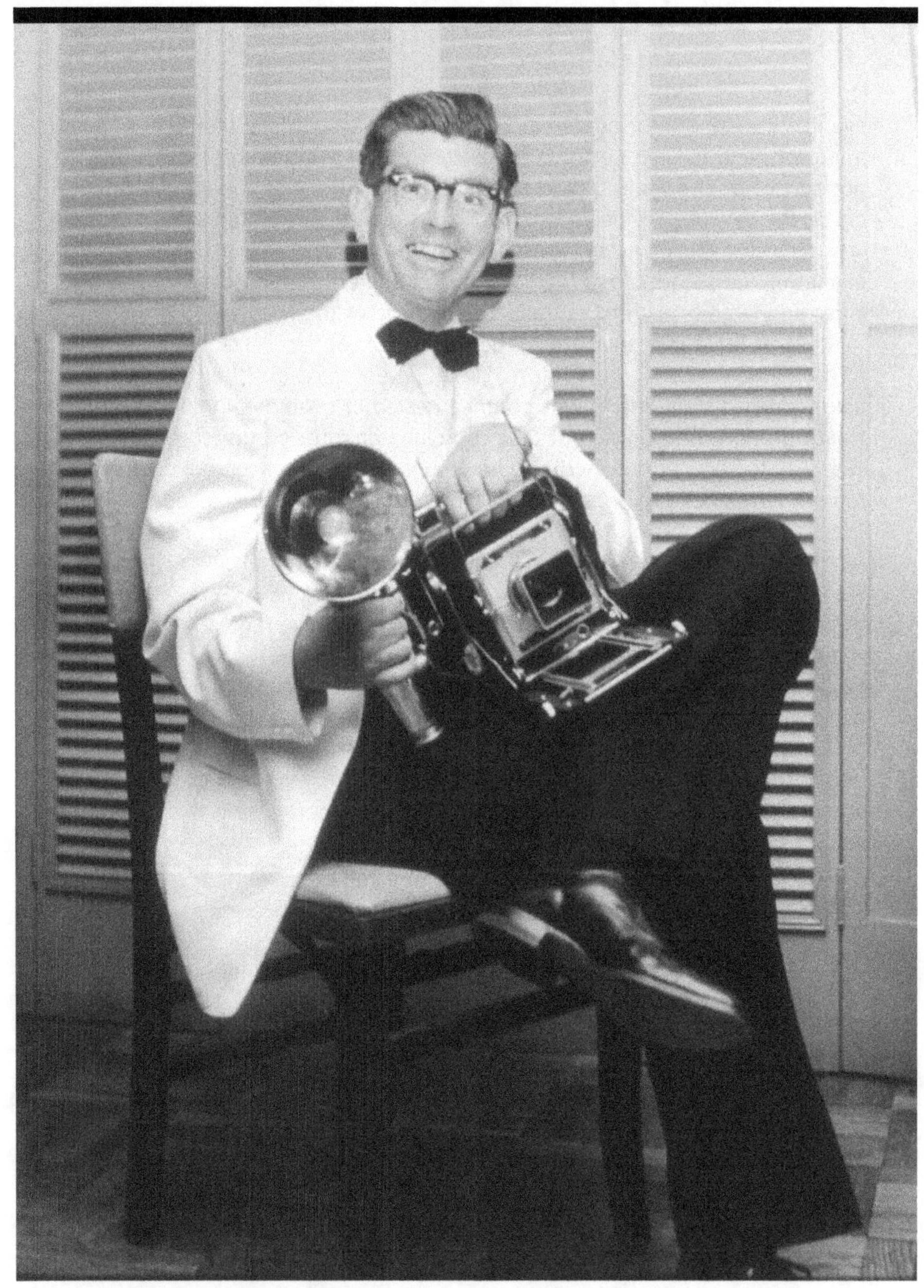

Leo J. "Scoop" Leeburn at age 34, having fun while capturing photos at a wedding on May 1, 1954.

Scoop Leeburn's
LOST CITY

by Mary Harbst

Leo J. "Scoop" Leeburn was born in Pawtucket, Rhode Island, in 1921. In 1943, at the age of 22, Leo and his family moved to Boise. Leo immediately fell in love with Boise's downtown and embraced the area as his personal territory, where he was often seen walking with his camera day or night. When he first arrived in Boise, he enjoyed riding on patrol with officers from the Boise and Ada County police forces. As a result, he was typically the first person to photograph the scenes of accidents and fires, earning him the friendly nickname of "Scoop." He worked for the Ada County Sheriff's Department for several years. Scoop's freelance photography included city nightlife, weddings, parades, sporting events, local buildings and city views. His pictures were frequently printed in the local newspapers. Even though Scoop was a shy man, he quickly became very popular. Many Boiseans enjoyed chatting with him as he strolled the streets, and were thrilled when he wanted to take their picture. In 1999, Scoop's photos that captured the changes in Boise from the 1940s to the 1980s were displayed at the Idaho Historical Museum. Scoop continued his freelance work until he passed away in 2002 at the age of 81. The photos in this chapter depict not only the "lost city" of Boise's downtown, but also display the insight Scoop possessed in capturing images of the area.

"Scoop's" pictures demonstrate the rich history of Boise's downtown, and depict the vibrant city of the past, the "lost city." Some of the buildings have been preserved, but many that were reusable were regrettably razed. Boise is trying to learn from its past mistakes and the irreversible damages of tearing down historic buildings by placing a focus on urban, mixed-use, sustainable development.

● ● ●

Mary Harbst is a graduate of Highland High School in Pocatello. A freshman studying nursing, she will graduate in 2013 and then plans to work as a nurse in the Boise area.

What are the most important aspects of a "livable" city?

"A city is livable if its focus is on urban, mixed-use, sustainable development that will protect open spaces and create a desirable place for people and wildlife alike. There must be amenities that include jobs, transportation, stores, restaurants and a variety of entertainment."

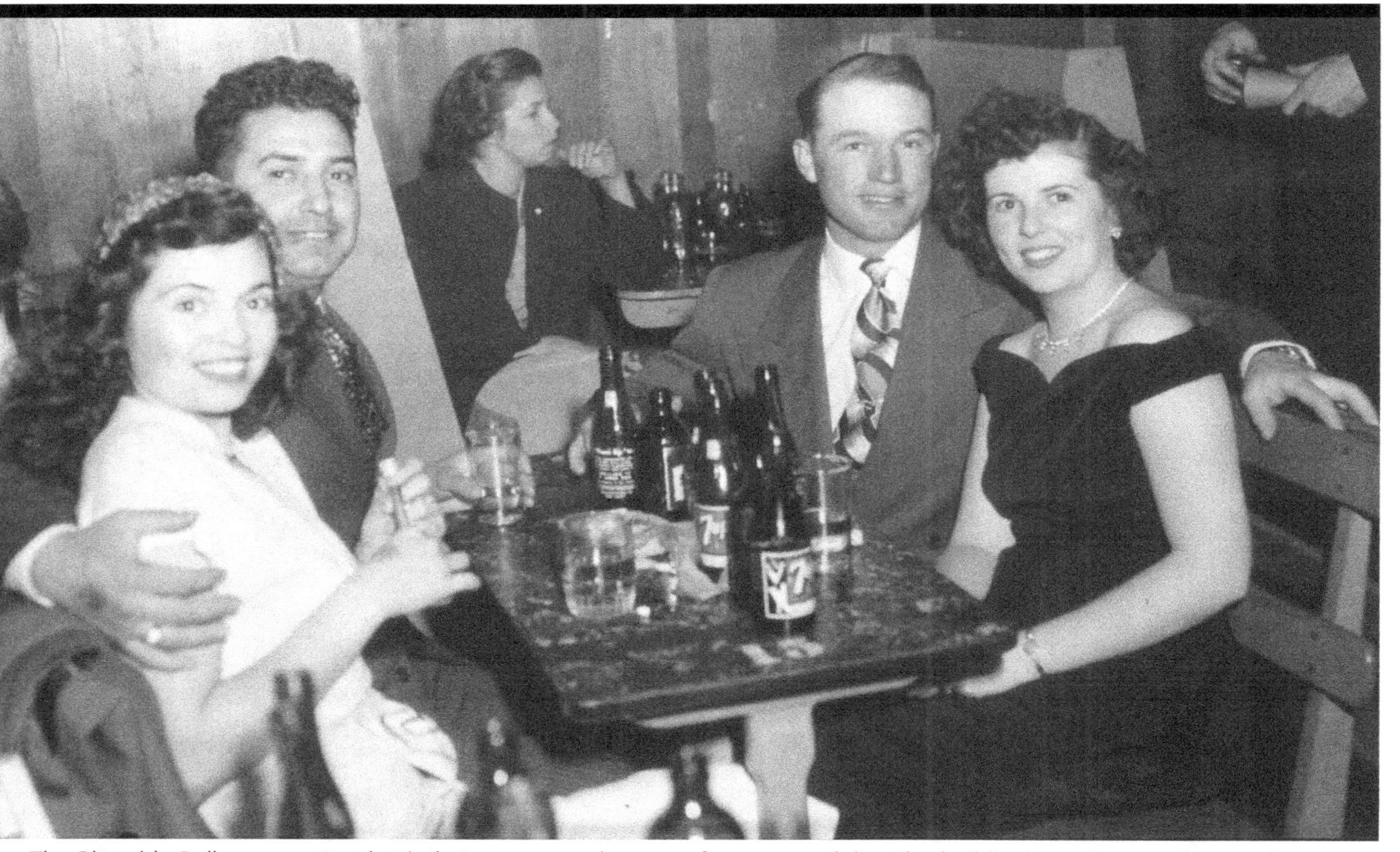

The Riverside Ballroom on South Ninth Street was a hot spot for young adults. The building now houses the Mardi Gras Ballroom.

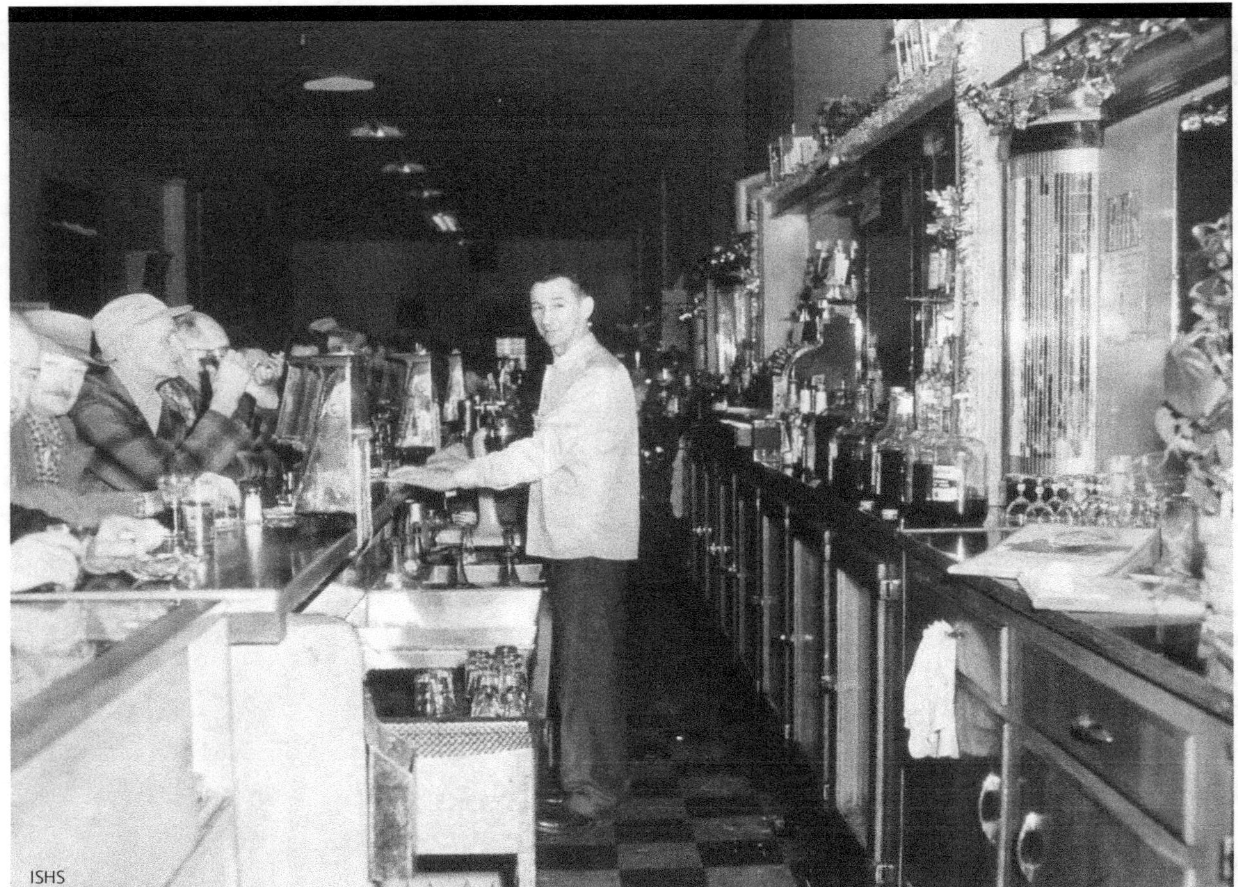

ISHS

Bartender serves customers at Main Street's Pastime Sportsmen's Club, 1967.

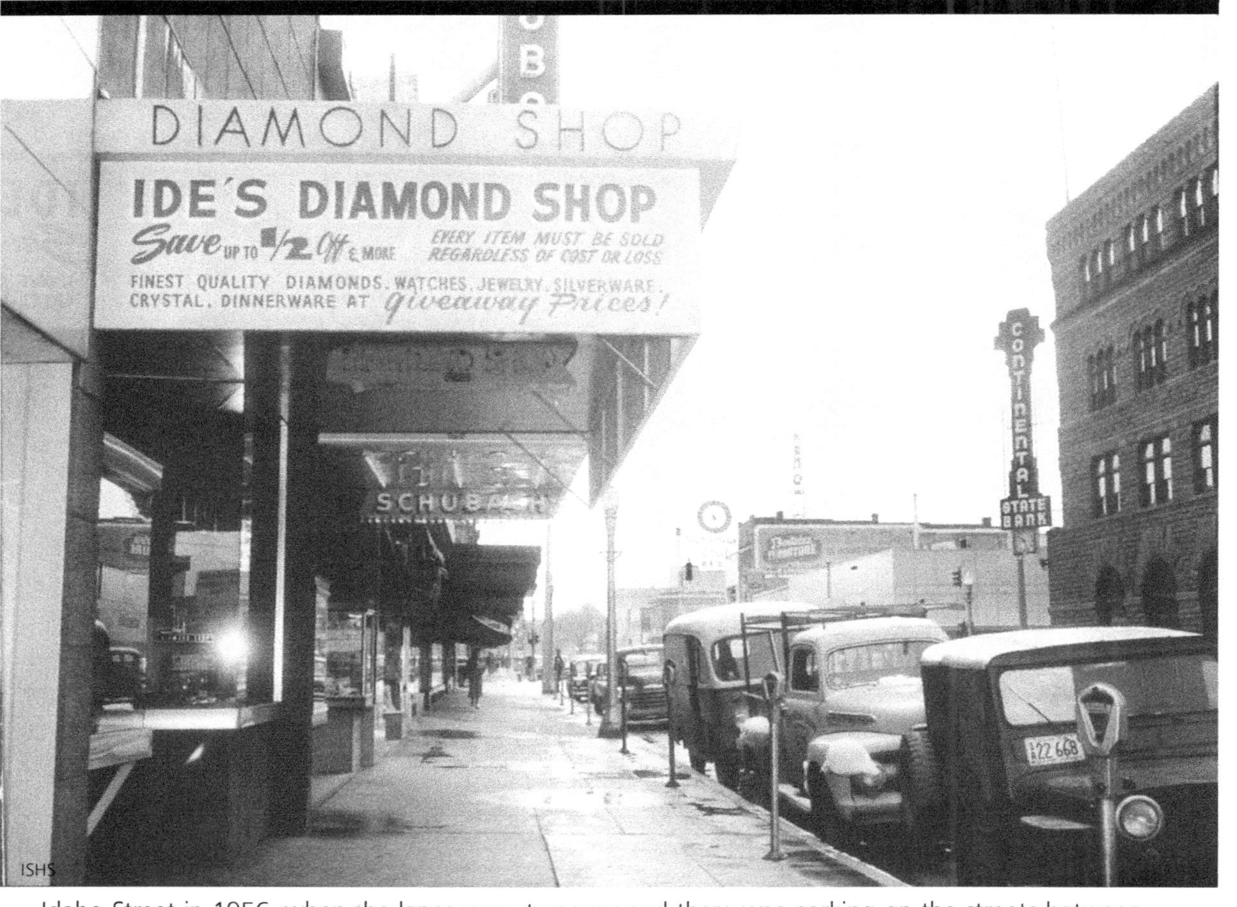

Idaho Street in 1956, when the lanes were two-way and there was parking on the streets between Eighth and Ninth.

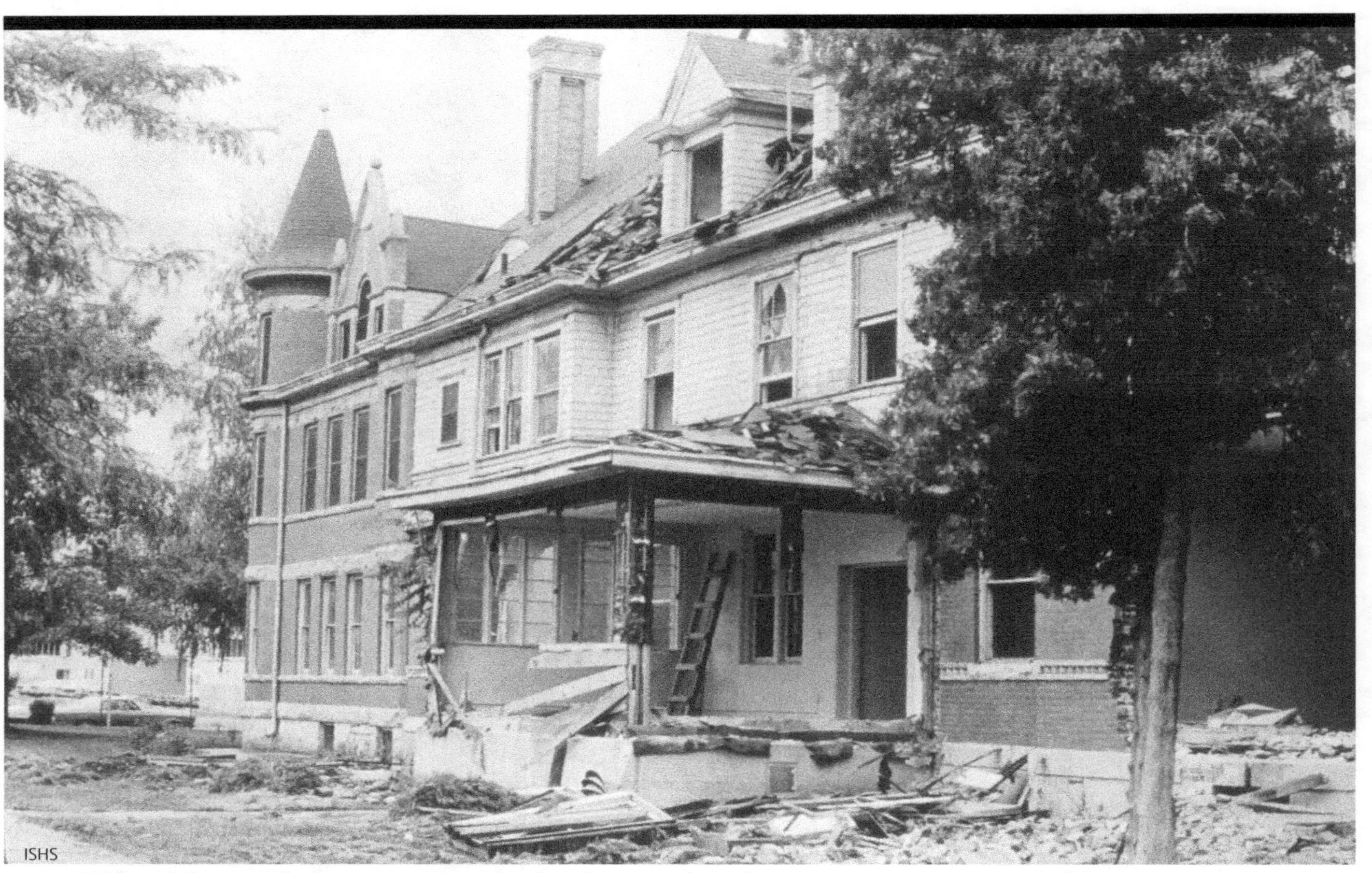

In 1976, at Fifth and State, the St. Alphonsus building was demolished. A state government building now occupies the site.

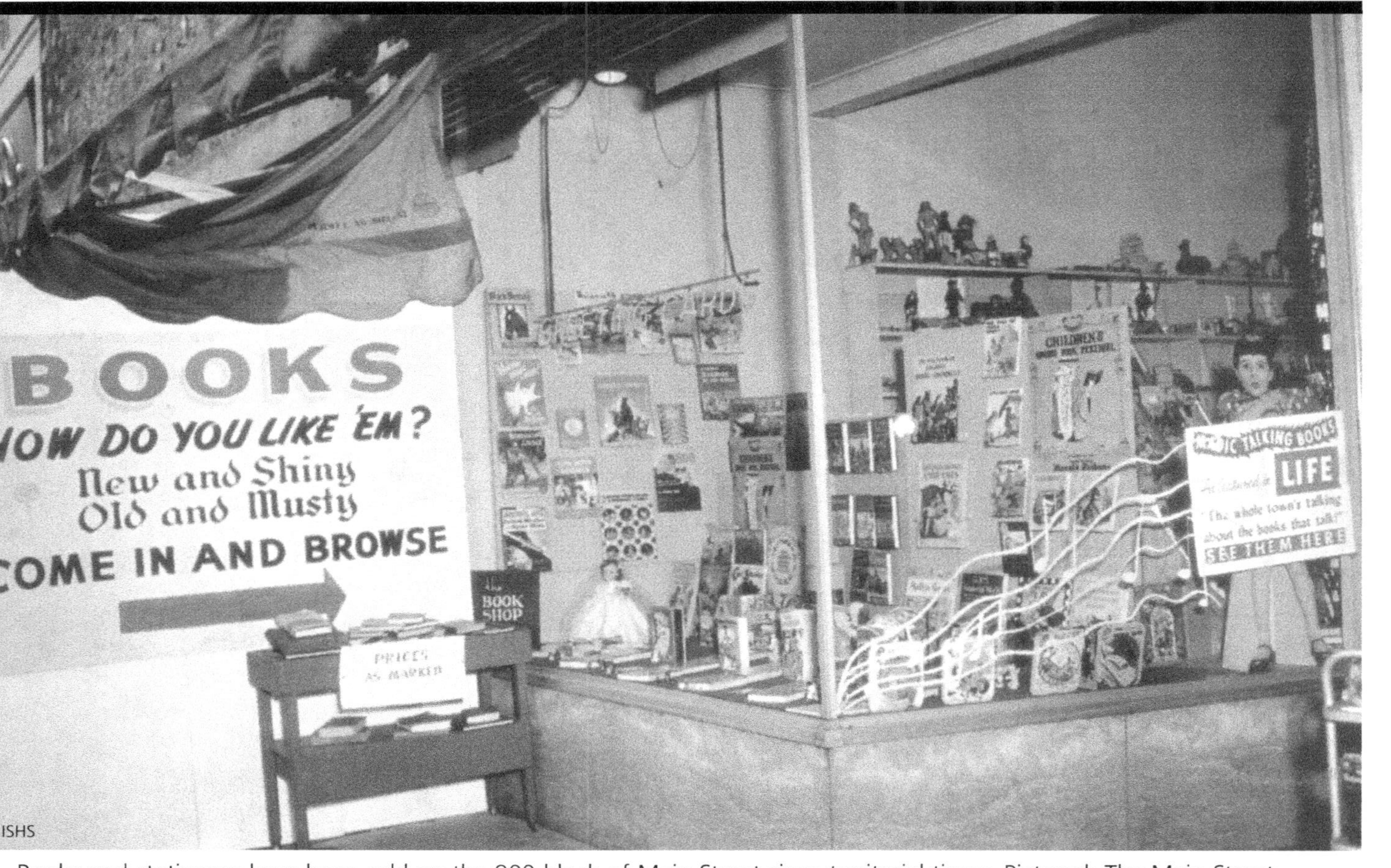

ISHS

Books and stationary have been sold on the 900 block of Main Street since territorial times. Pictured: The Main Street Book Shop in the James Pinney Building, 1955.

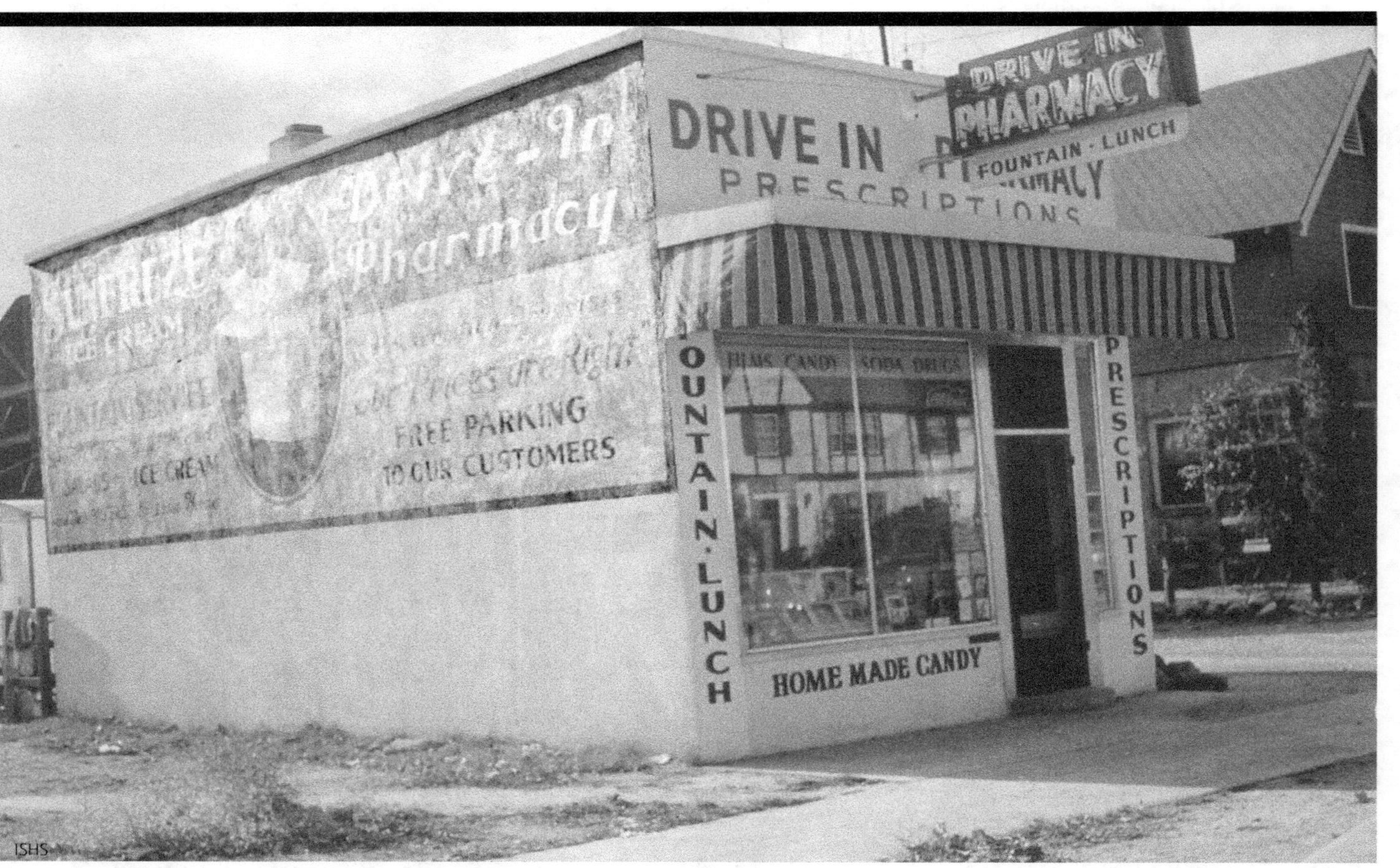

ISHS

Boise merchants adapted to the automobile as suburbanization sapped the downtown core. Pictured: a downtown drive-in pharmacy, about 1960.

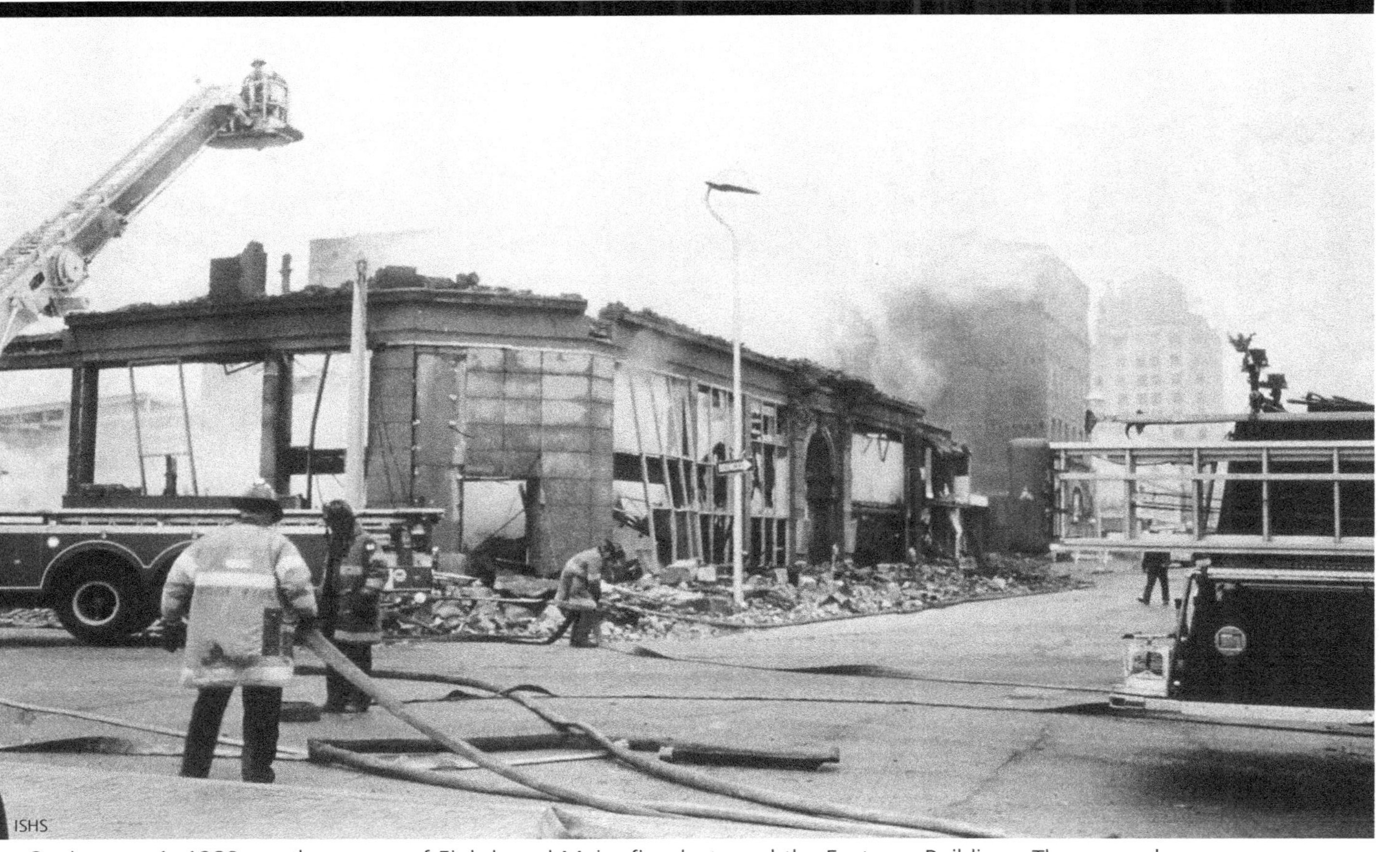

ISHS

On January 1, 1989, on the corner of Eighth and Main, fire destroyed the Eastman Building. The corner has remained vacant ever since.

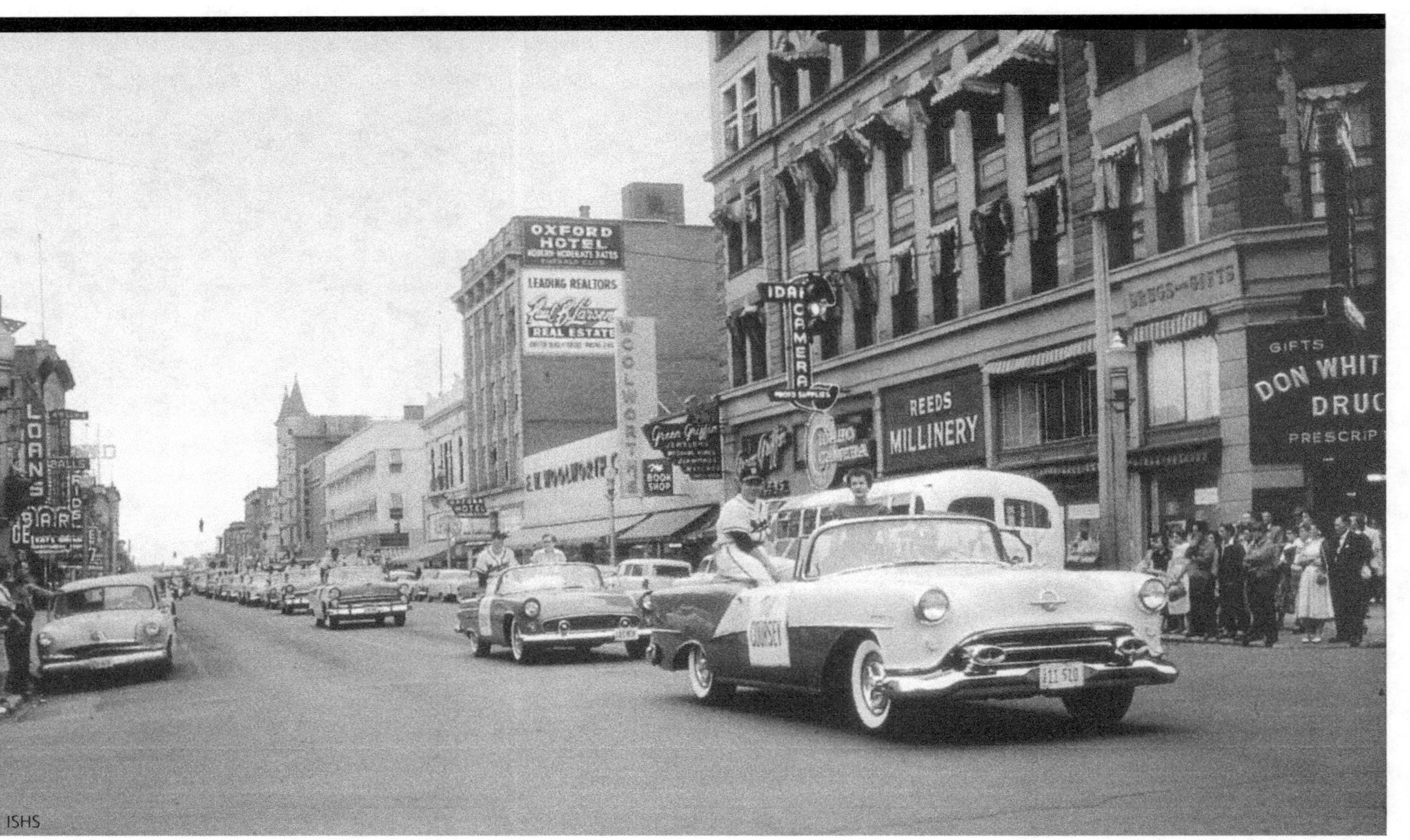

On April 25, 1956, baseball players paraded past the 800 block of Main Street in an era when hotels and department stores still dominated commercial downtown.

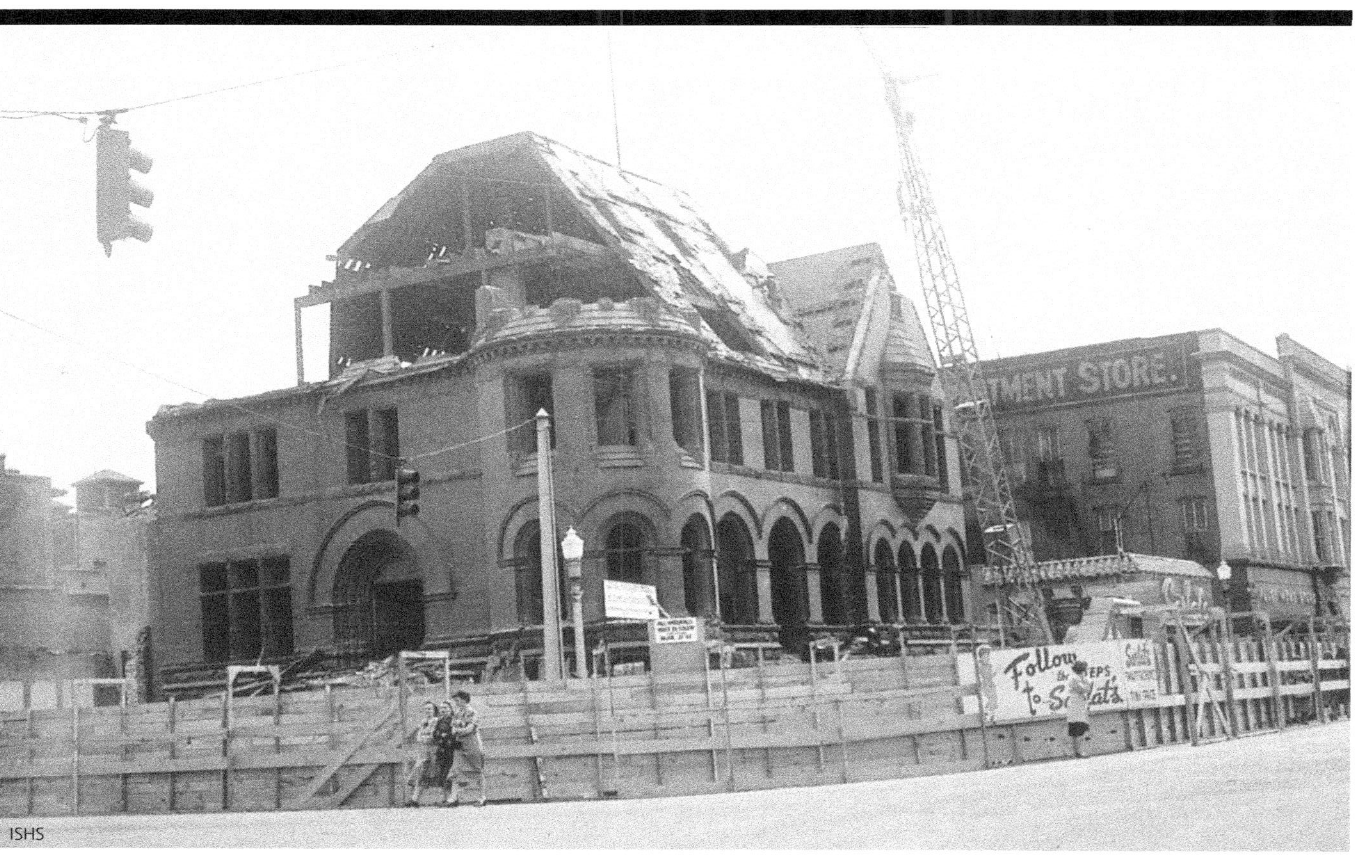

ISHS

Tearing down Boise City Hall, 1953. A flat-roof Skaggs drug store replaced the brick and sandstone landmark.

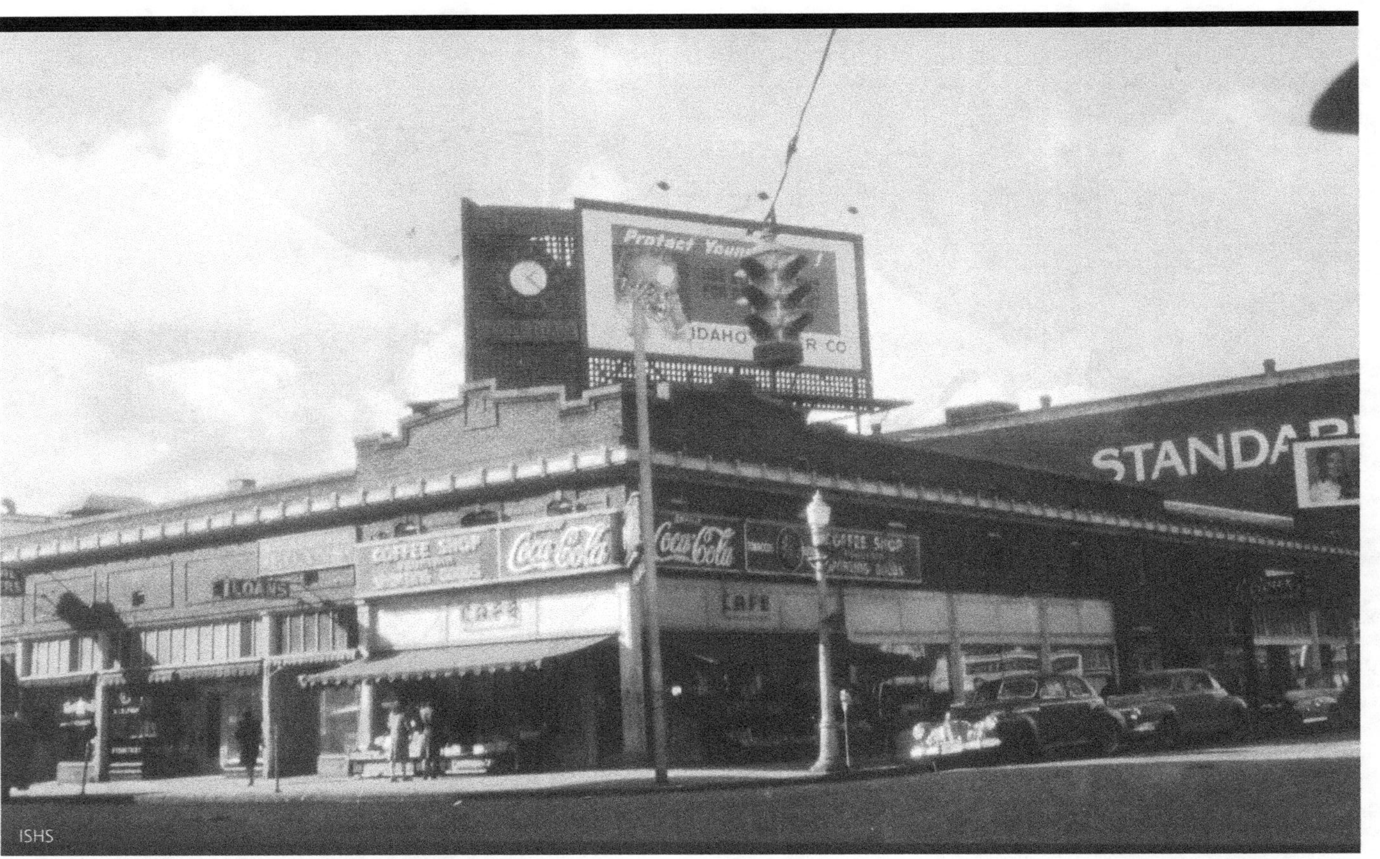

The Southeast corner of Eighth at Bannock, 1949. Bobby-soxers played juke box music at the corner soda fountain.

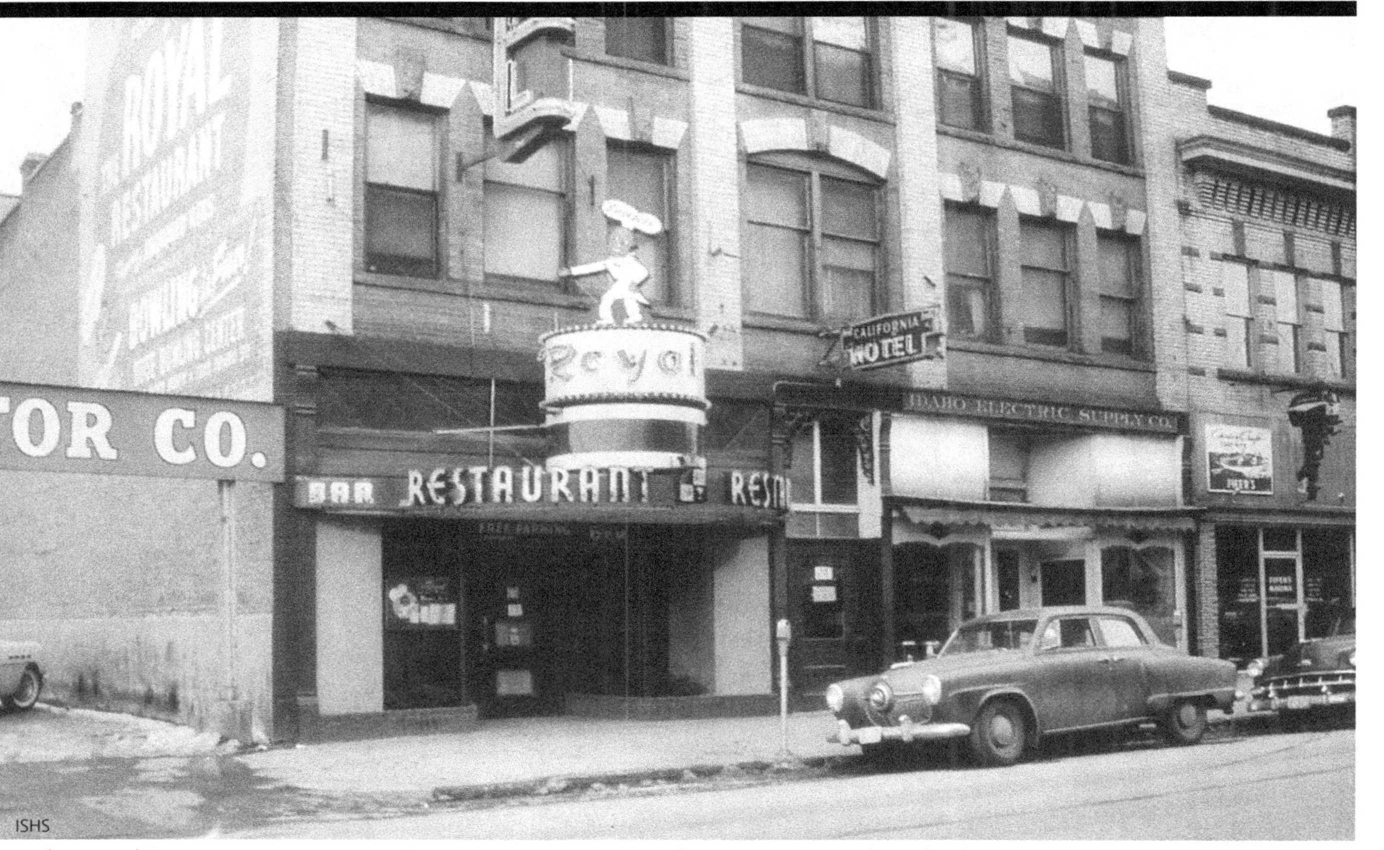

ISHS

The Royal Restaurant at 1112 Main Street was once Boise's premier prom-date destination. Luxury condominiums now occupy the site.

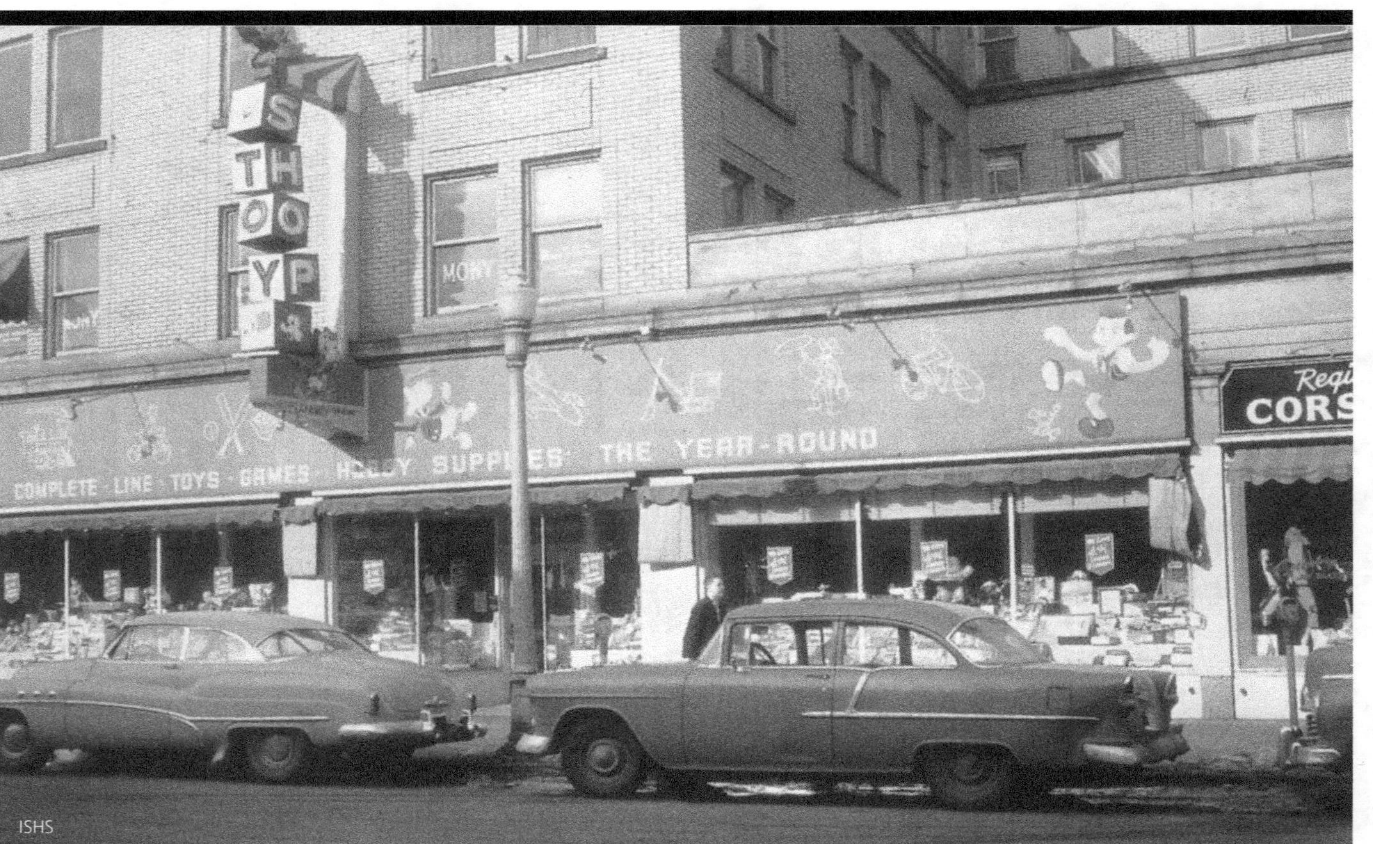

Retail once thrived in the 1902 Gem-Noble Building. Today the building houses restaurants and luxury condominiums.

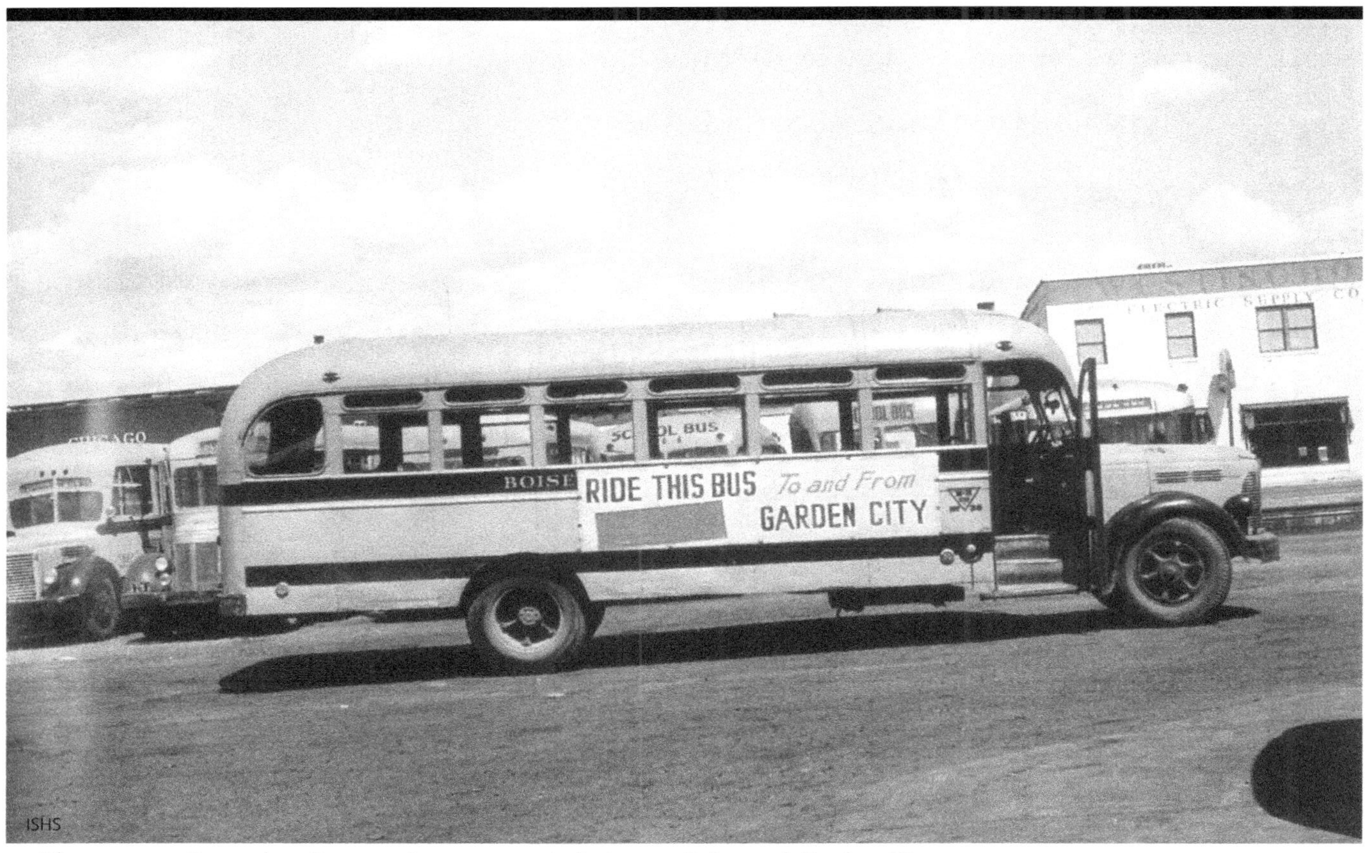

There was a time when it was a long commute between Boise and Garden City.

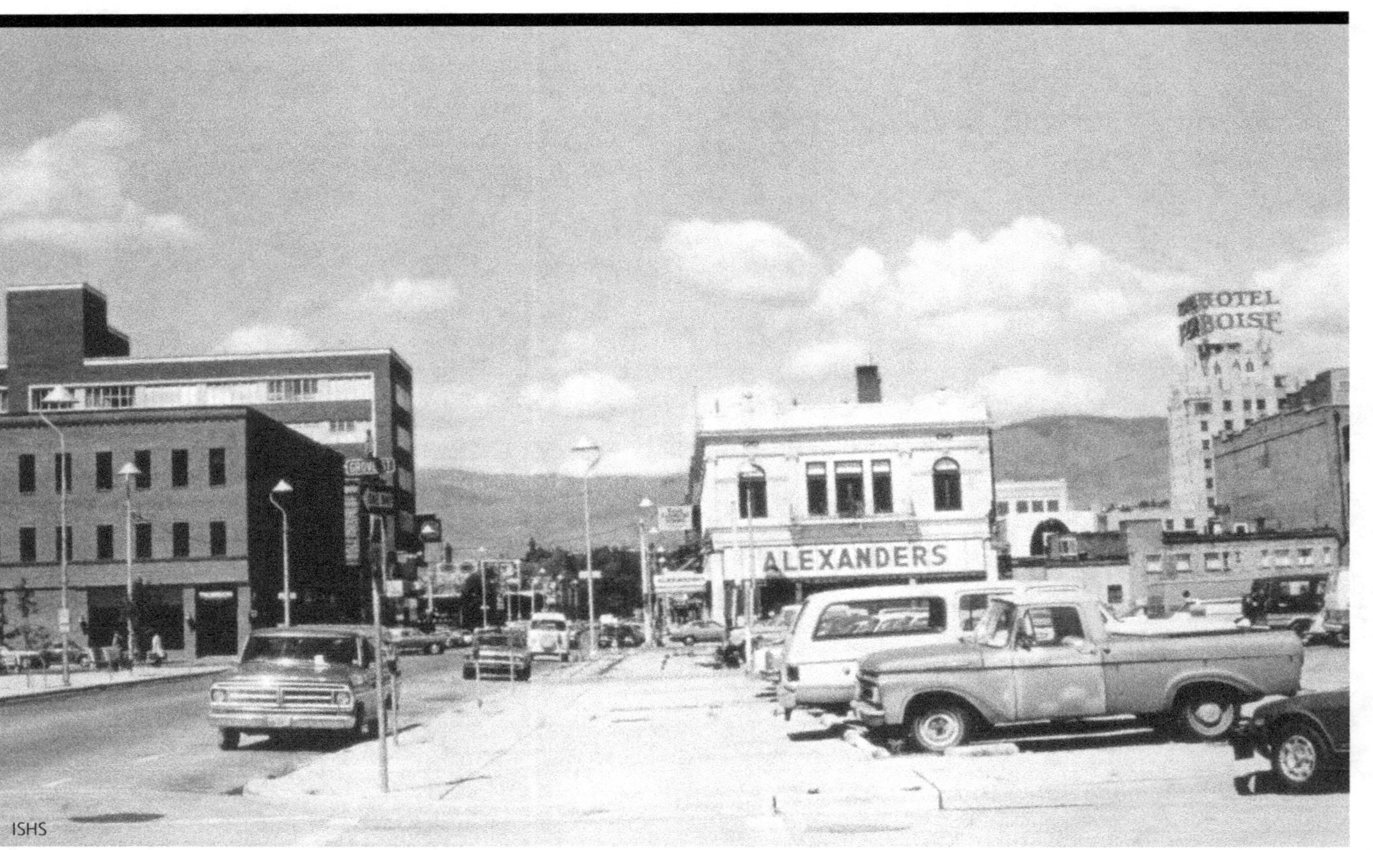

The parking lot to the right of Ninth Street is now the location for the Wells Fargo Bank and the Grove Plaza, a community gathering place and location for special events.

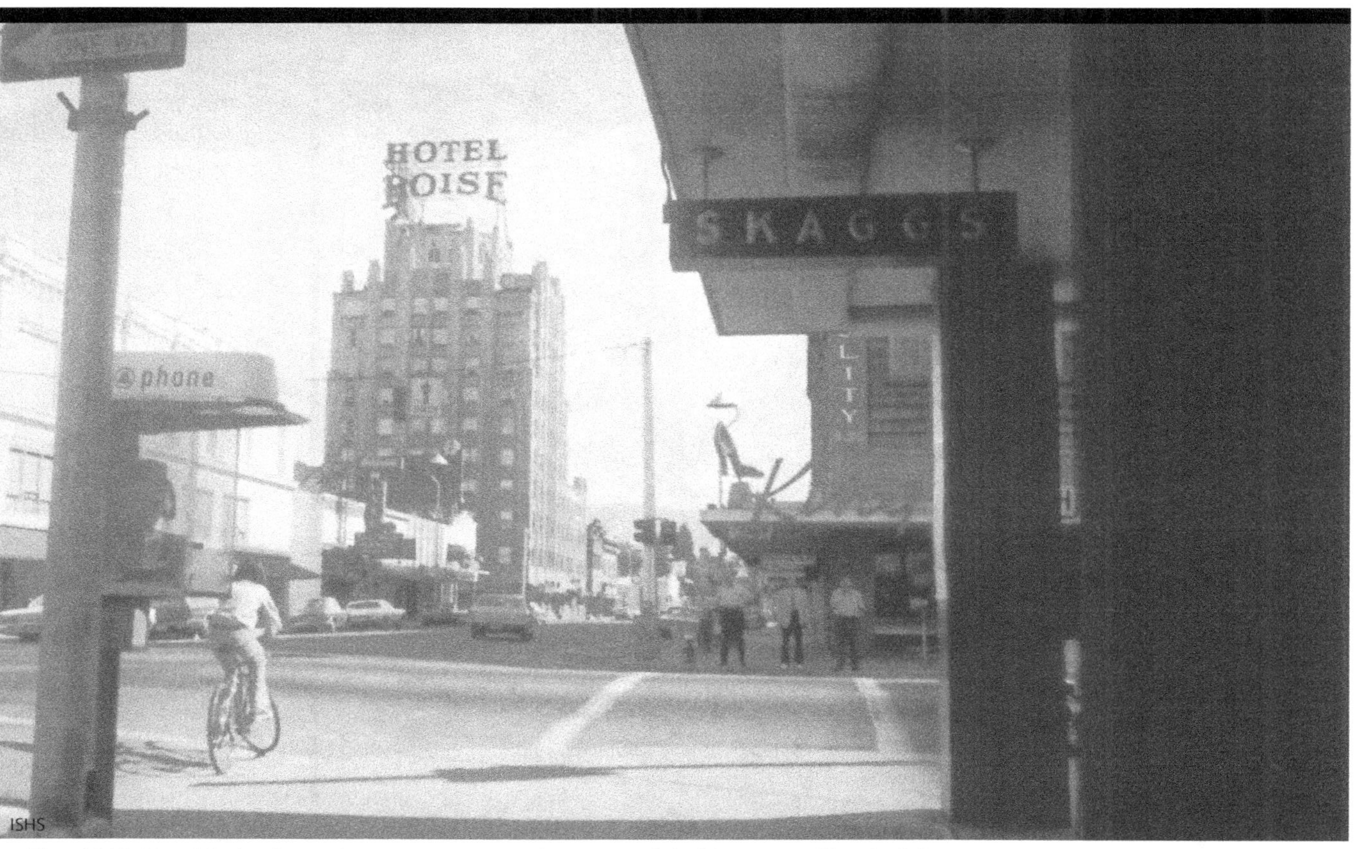

The 1929 Hotel Boise brought Art Deco to Boise. Remodeled into an office building with a roof-top restaurant in 1979, the hotel lost its signature neon sign and Deco pillar crown.

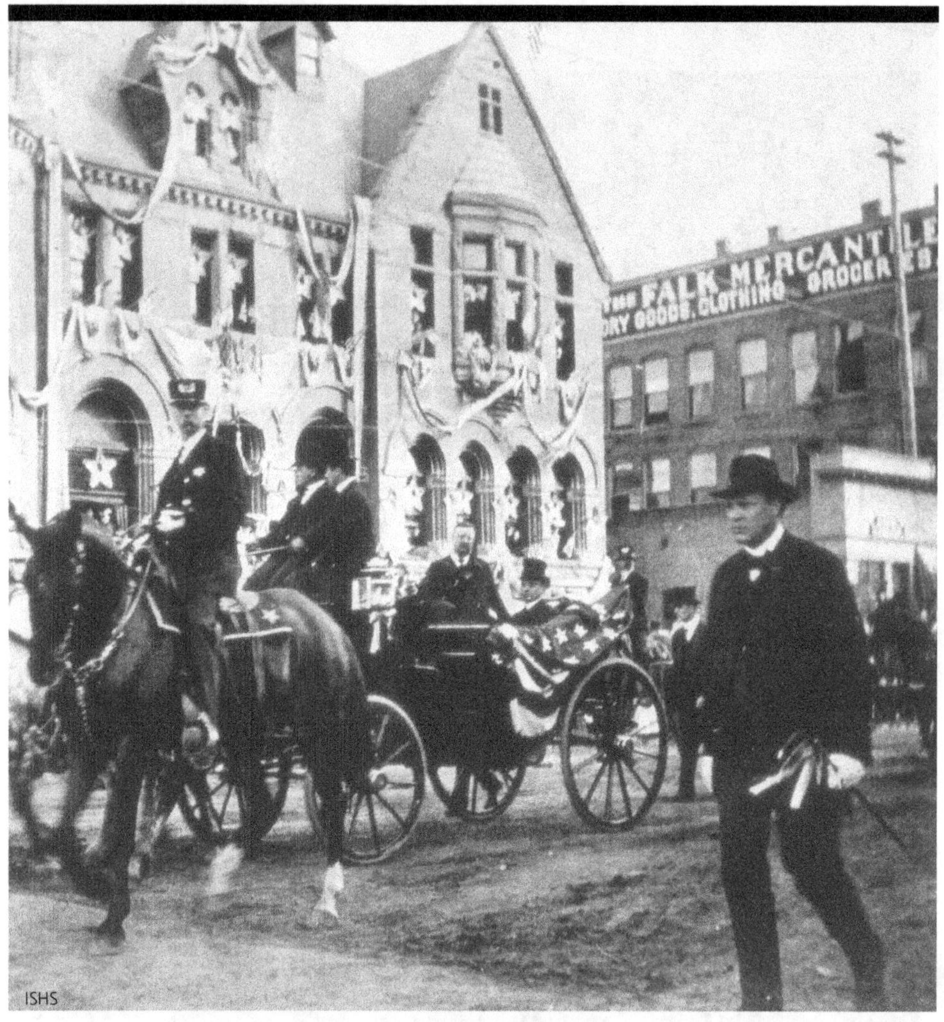

ISHS

President Theodore Roosevelt parades north on Eighth Street past Boise's Romanesque Revival City Hall, 1903.

Urban

CROSSROADS

by Jacey Brain

The downtown intersection of 8th and Idaho streets—just a stone's throw from City Hall, the Boise Convention Center, several of the state's largest banks and dozens of retail stores and restaurants—is the urbane hub of Boise. Its street scene reflects Boise at its citified best—an eclectic mingle of counterculture teen-agers, button-down bankers/lawyers and North End vegans, all going their separate ways, yet brought together on this busy patch of downtown real estate. But as contemporary as the 8th and Idaho scene is, three of its four corners are occupied by historic buildings whose rich heritage and classic aesthetics date back to the dirt-street days before the automobile.

The Mode Building and Fidelity Building, both former department stores, sit on two of the corners. The Simplot Building, once the home of Boise City National Bank, occupies the third. Until 1953, the fourth corner featured a Romanesque-style City Hall where the Capitol Terrace parking garage and retail complex now sit. In addition to a variety of shops and restaurants, these buildings include professional and office space. Adjacent blocks feature residential space, and a proposed apartment complex above the Capitol Terrace could eventually come to fruition. Through mixed use—a combination of retail, office and residential space—the corner of 8th and Idaho serves as a perfect example of "smart growth" in Boise. The preservation and mixed-use development of classic buildings is at the heart of the block's success, and can serve as a template for others across the city.

The intersection hasn't always been the lively, people-centered place it is today. In fact, it witnessed one of the most regretful eras in Boise's city planning, a time when a large segment of the historic downtown fell to the wrecking ball in the name of "urban renewal." But, unlike many to the south, the intersection survived intact and eventually benefitted from the subsequent emphasis on the redevelopment of existing downtown buildings. The urban renewal saga began in the mid-1960s when Boise's central downtown suffered from disinvestment and suburbs began to sprawl at the edges of Boise. A civic task group developed a central business district plan in 1964 that called for a process of urban renewal, including the clearance and redevelopment of downtown's blighted areas. The City Council adopted the plan and created the Boise Redevelopment Agency (B.R.A.) in 1965 after passage of Idaho's Urban Renewal Law. Between 1965 and 1969, the B.R.A. (now called the Capital City Development Corporation) surveyed the area and then acquired and cleared buildings deemed to be beyond rehabilitation or in the way of the large, multi-block regional shopping center planned for the central business district. Using federal urban renewal funding, the B.R.A. acquired 12 blocks and cleared six between 1965 and 1974. Four city blocks cleared for the shopping center became parking lots. As the B.R.A. began to demolish historic downtown buildings, ordinary citizens and prominent Boise residents alike condemned the activity. Senator Frank Church urged the agency to "...save what remains of downtown Boise before the bulldozers run completely amuck." While the B.R.A. succeeded in completing some projects during this time—most notably the new Boise City Hall and the tall U.S. Bank building—the downtown shopping center never advanced beyond the planning stages. The B.R.A worked with five major shopping center developers over the years, none of which worked out due to the unresponsiveness and unwillingness of major retailers to commit to the project. When the last of the five developers resigned in May 1985, the B.R.A. asked the Regional/Urban Design Assistance Team (R/UDAT) at the American Institute of Architects to study Boise's downtown area and develop a new concept plan. Following the advice of the R/UDAT, the B.R.A. abandoned the proposed shopping mall and took the plans for the central business district in a new direction that called for mixed-use development and the reintroduction of regulated private development. The R/UDAT stated that the development of downtown Boise "must pull together people and factions fragmented by two decades of the redevelopment struggle," and that "it must succeed in

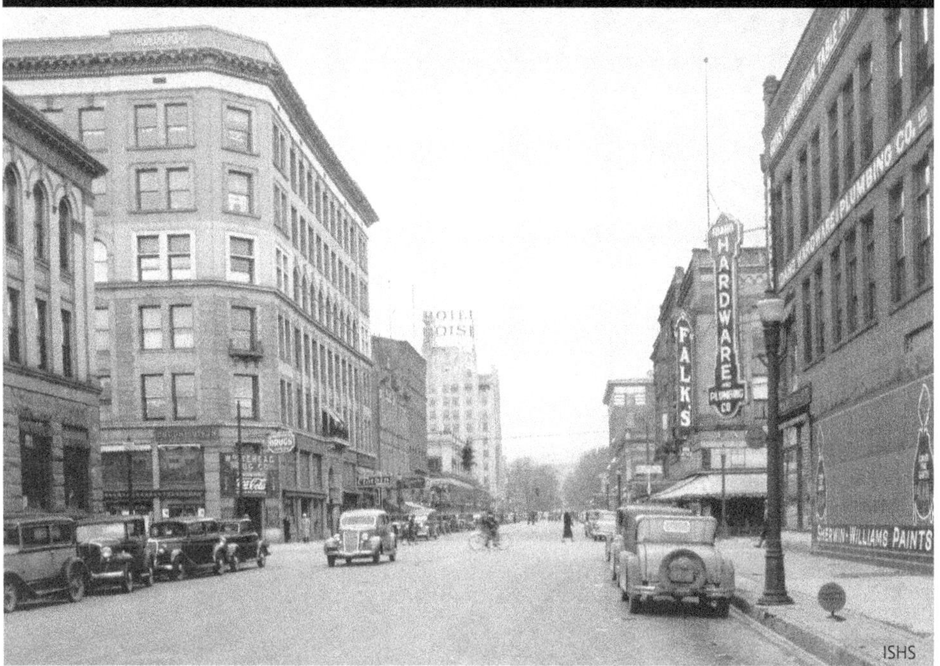

Photographer R. Harold Sigler captured the commercial vitality of Eighth Street, looking north from Main Street, about 1930.

blueprinting a redeveloped city core with business, entertainment and recreational opportunities that will provide the sense of identity Boiseans have missed." In the plan, the R/UDAT suggested that the "Eighth Street Mall," or 8th Street between Front Street and Bannock, should be the focus of new development in downtown Boise's core.

The R/UDAT plan for the outdoor mall on 8th Street suggested that retail space should line the street at ground level and the landscaping should be informal, connecting the Boise River and the Greenbelt to the Capitol Building. Outdoor entertainment and cultural and recreational activities should be interspersed along the way. In 1986, the Boise City Council adopted a new plan for downtown that envisioned Eighth Street as a pedestrian-friendly zone with an emphasis on open public space. It called for street trees and iron tree grates, appropriate lighting and street furniture, and furnishings for the whole width of the street. Since 1987, the streetscapes around 8th and Idaho have undergone major renovations. The wider side-

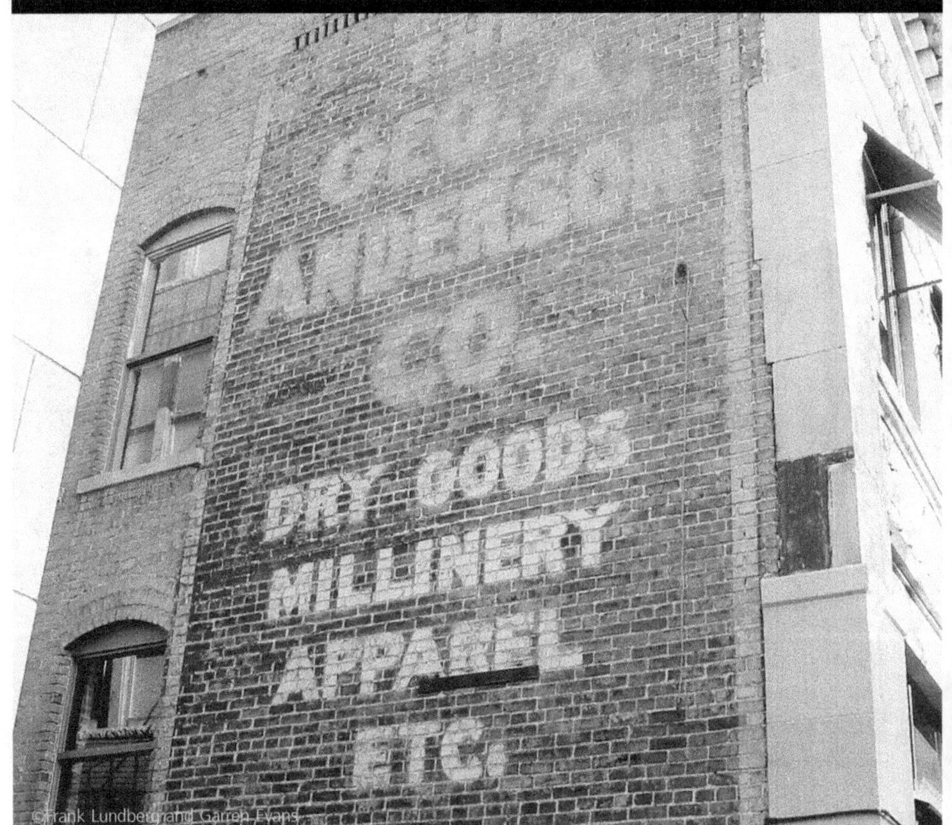

Service alleys contribute to the walkability of the urban renewal district. Pictured: alleyway ghost sign behind the Fidelity Building, 2009.

walks along 8th Street between Idaho and Bannock now feature extensive patio space for the restaurants on the block. The streetscape also includes trees, benches, planters, bicycle racks and even public art. Although the street did not become an auto-free zone, it is open only to slow traffic and street parking is limited. The improvements allow for optimal mixed use. Several restaurants take advantage of the upgraded sidewalks that line both sides of 8th Street. According to CCDC Executive Director Phil Kushlan, all new plans for development in downtown Boise call for the sidewalks to be designed to encourage people to walk and spend more time. Kushlan says that the goal is to "extend activity downtown beyond 8 to 5, rather than rolling up the sidewalks at 5 o'clock." Special events, such as the Capital City Public Market, with its blend of local art, food and agricultural products, draw thousands of people to 8th Street each weekend from early spring to late fall.

The three historic buildings that anchor the 8th and Idaho intersection came through Boise's "urban renewal" era of the 1960s and 1970s unscathed as visible reminders of Boise's past, yet they are vitally immersed in the present. The stories of their early years are testaments to the city's rich heritage of entrepreneurship and civic pride. Developers used sandstone from Table Rock Quarry to construct the Boise City National Bank, founded by Henry Wadsworth and Alfred Eoff, in 1891-92 on the southwest corner of the intersection. The team of John Tourtellotte and Charles Frederick Hummel, along with James King, designed the building. Tourtellotte and Hummel designed almost 200 Boise buildings. In 1905, Boise approved the addition of a new story and an annex to the building, costing $80,000. The bank ceased operation during the Great Depression on Aug. 1, 1932. After the bank closed, over the years the building has been home to many tenants, including offices for Idaho Power, J.R. Simplot Co., lawyers, accountants, architects, real estate companies and the CCDC. In 1978, the building was named to the National Park Service's Register of Historic Places. Developer Rick Peterson completed a $4 million renovation in 1993, attracting a variety of tenants that includes restaurants, retail outlets and offices. An outdoor dining area in front of the former bank contributes to the intersection's lively atmosphere.

The Mode Building stands at the northwest corner of 8th and Idaho. Completed in 1895, the building housed the Mode, Ltd., a department store for almost 100 years until it closed in 1991. Before the Mode's construction, a small store called the Palace Meat Market stood at the corner. In its early days, the Mode block brought high-end and specialty shopping to downtown Boise. Harry Falk, a member of the family that established Falk's Department Store, hired Boise-based developer John Broadbent to build the Mode's three-story building, which featured picture windows on each floor. Several other locally-owned department stores made their homes in downtown Boise during the heyday of the Mode, including Falk's, the Bazaar and C.C. Anderson's, all of which the Mode outlasted. Despite the continued success of the store, Falk and his partners sold the business to J.J. Chapman in 1938. Chapman's wife, Ethel, began managing the store after he died only four years later. Fire engulfed the Mode's interior on June 18, 1958. The disaster attracted thousands of people, who watched as fire and water destroyed everything inside the store. Chapman held a reopening ceremony for the rebuilt store nine months later. In 1969, she sold the Mode to James Ruark, the manager of Falk's. As soon as the store opened, downtown shoppers quickly grew fond of second-floor Mode Tea Room, beginning a long tradition of dining in the Mode Building that continues today. In 1988, Ruark completely upgraded all four floors and expanded retail space. He turned down an offer to move to the Boise Towne Square mall, and instead purchased the building from the B.R.A., which had obtained the property in 1978 during the urban renewal project. Despite his satisfaction with the remodeling, Ruark put the Mode, Ltd. up for sale in January 1991. But that October he announced that the landmark Boise store would close by the end of the year, stating that the business was not profitable enough to remain open. The Mode Building was empty for a few years following the store's closure. In 1994, after another major interior renovation (and demolition), tenants returned, and today the building includes a mix of restaurants and retail businesses. Many residents credited the area's recent business boom to the reopening of the Mode Building.

Across from the Mode, the sandstone Fidelity Building, formerly called the Montandon Building after builder August F. Montandon, has functioned as a mixed-use property for more than a century. Architect J.W. Smith, who designed the Montandon in the Romanesque Revival style, built several buildings in Baltimore before the Boise project. In late 1908, the $30,000 building became the new home of the Anderson-Blomquist department store. Prior to that, Sanborn maps indicate that the corner was home to several small businesses, including a barber, a fish market and a hardware store turned candy store. The Anderson-Blomquist store held its grand opening in the new building on Jan. 15, 1909, but in 1927 the store closed and one year later the building became home to the Fidelity Loan and Investment Company. Although the company was in business only until 1932, it put a "Fidelity" sign on the second floor and since then the structure has been known as the Fidelity Building. For the next 55 years the building saw many tenants come and go, including drug stores, government agencies, retail outlets and non-profit organizations.

In 1972, the National Park Service added the Union Block and Fidelity Building as one piece of architecture to the National Register of Historic Places. In 1986, consultants advised the B.R.A. that a restoration of the Fidelity-Union Block would be economically practical. Planners expressed

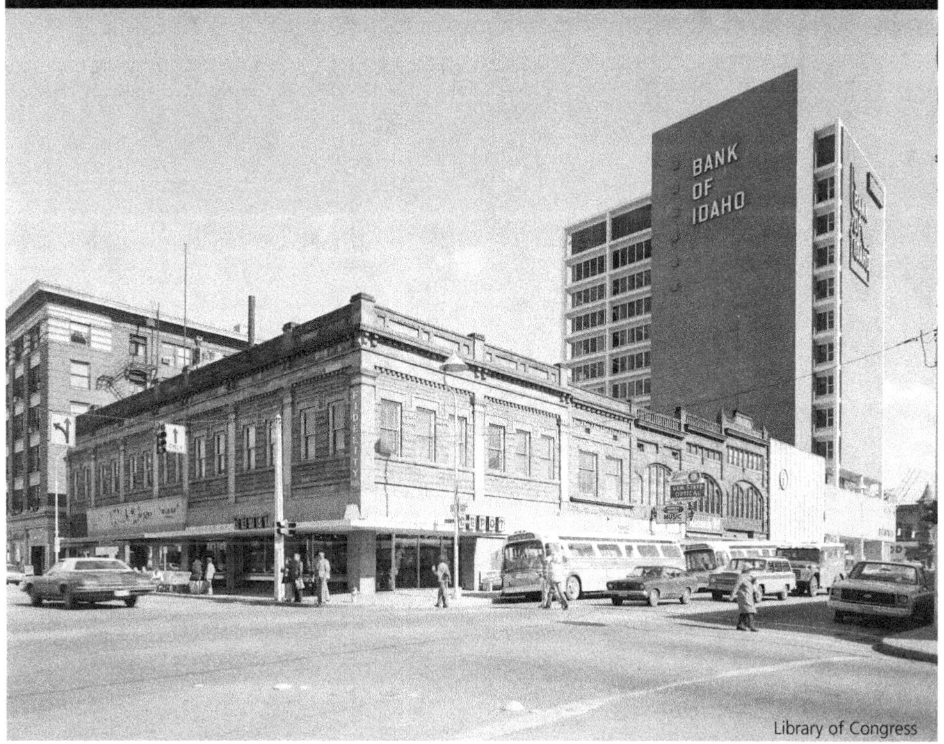

The 1908 Fidelity Building abuts the Union Block on the northeast corner of Eighth and Idaho, about 1978.

immediate interest in the project, even though reports anticipated the restoration would cost $3.6 million and it would take an estimated four years to fill all vacancies with tenants. Investors Gary Christensen and James Tomlinson purchased the Fidelity Building, refurbishing it during their first year (1993) and operating it for only five years. They sold it to David Almquist, president and CEO of California-based marketing firm The Designory, Inc. Today the building is home to several restaurants that credit outdoor patio dining combined with the revitalized downtown for their success. Re-use of the historic Fidelity Building brought a new energy and audience to 8th and Idaho, and contributed to the block's present day mixed-use atmosphere.

The Capitol Terrace, the only contemporary building on the corner of 8th and Idaho, was the site of the former Boise City Hall, a Romanesque

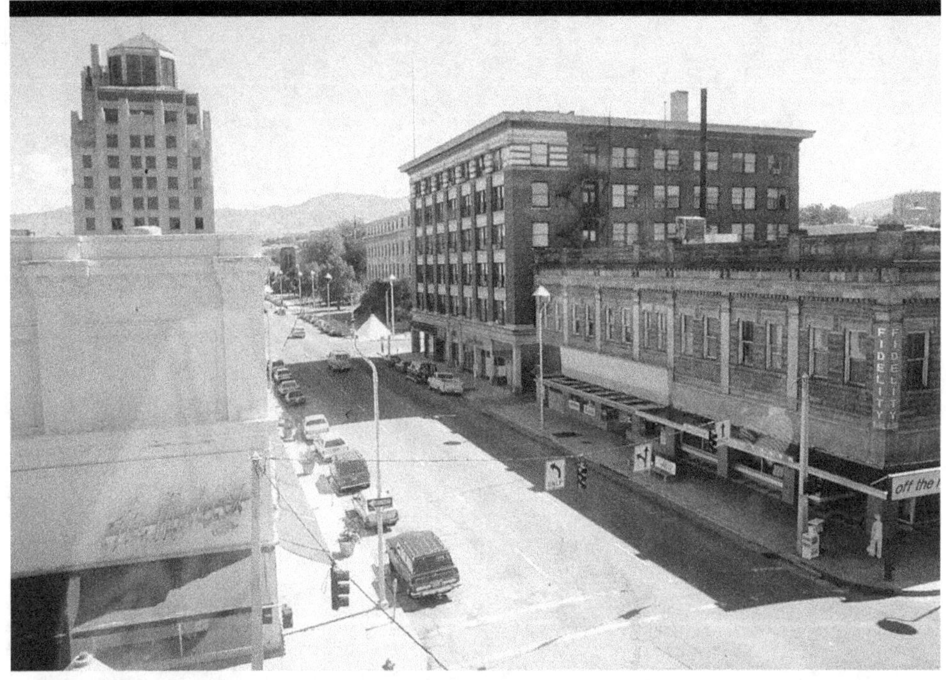

North-bound traffic dominated Eighth Street, about 1980. Barren, treeless sidewalks discouraged walking.

Revival building designed by German architect James C. Paulsen and completed in 1893. The Boise City Council held its first meeting there on May 24, 1893, and it soon became the center of town celebrations and special events. The city put the City Hall up for sale in June 1948 after Mayor Potter P. Howard announced that city offices had outgrown the building. William Zeckendorf and the Webb and Knapp Corporation purchased the property after the building became vacant. After sitting empty for three years, it became a canteen for Boise military servicemen in 1951, and wrecking crews began dismantling the building in 1953. The space served as a temporary parking lot, and later a drug store occupied the corner for several years. In

1988, the CCDC took over the block and constructed the Capitol Terrace, a colorful mixed-use building that functions today as a parking garage enclosed by multi-level commercial space. The Capitol Terrace is one of several parking garages built between 1978-1990 in response to a R/UDAT survey

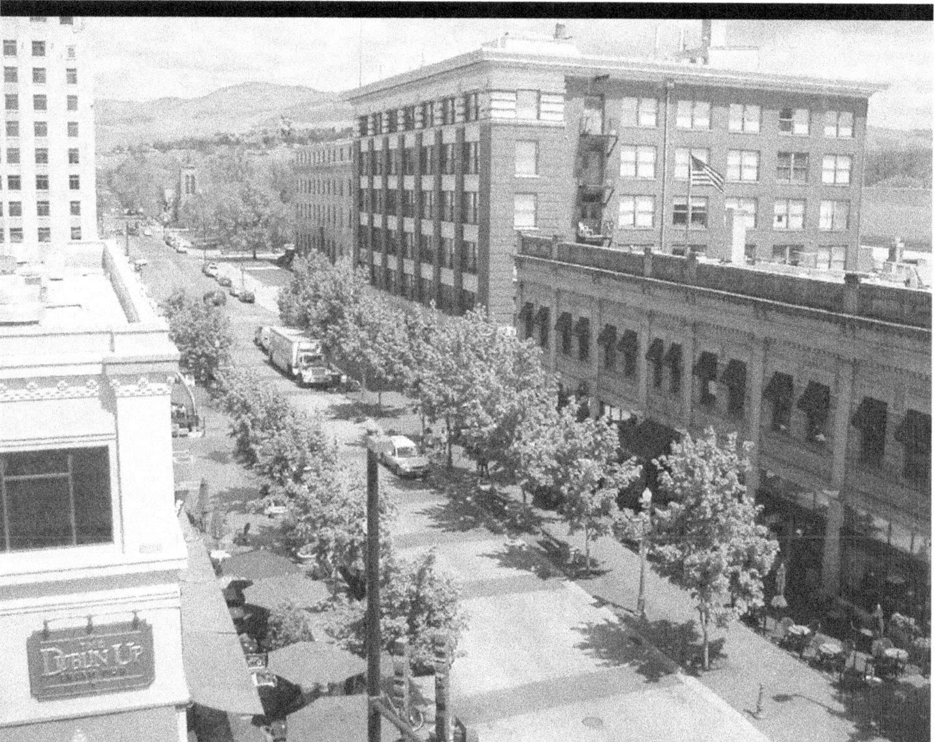

The 1990s remaking of Eighth Street included wide sidewalks, landscaping, benches, street art and patio seating.

that suggested that the surface parking lots downtown should be replaced with parking garages located near and integrated with new developments. Thus, the Capitol Terrace brings consolidated parking, an important element of mixed use, to the corner of 8th and Idaho.

While they have added character and interest to the intersection, the structures at 8th and Idaho lack one important element of mixed-use development—residential space. Although nearby locations such as the Idaho

Building and the Washington Mutual (now Chase) Building offer housing options in the heart of downtown Boise, the proposed Capitol Terrace Apartments above the garage structure could complete the 8th and Idaho mixed-use resume. Pam Sheldon, general contracts manager at CCDC, says

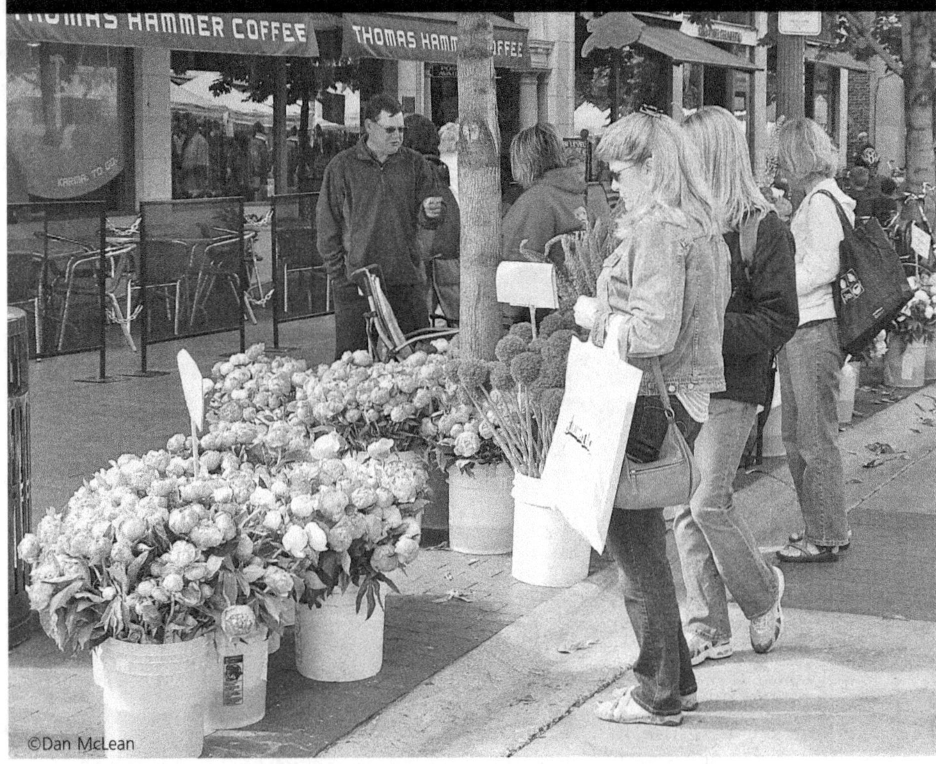

Crafts and produce lure crowds to the open-air Capital City Public Market. Pictured: buying flowers at Eighth and Bannock, 2009.

that traditional thinking paints city downtown areas as primarily centers for office and retail space. Instead, she explains, "Retail is a follower. Housing can do a lot to help other aspects of downtown development." CCDC-hired consultants found that downtown rated high in available jobs, retail, nightlife, recreation, schools and most importantly, demand for housing. So the CCDC began working with developers to consider locations for new residential space. Since 2006, 251 units of new downtown housing have been built in developments such as the Aspen Lofts, CitySide Lofts and the Royal Plaza, says Sheldon. In December 2005, developer Ken Howell of Parklane Management Co. proposed the construction of an 81-unit apartment complex to be built above the Capitol Terrace parking garage and retail building. The plans called for 57 studio or one-bedroom apartments to be targeted toward downtown workers and those with low incomes. One- or two-bedroom units to be rented at the normal market rate comprised the remainder of the complex. The downturn of the national economy and the decreased value of the property repeatedly delayed the development.

Continued preservation efforts and imaginative re-use of the buildings at 8th and Idaho have fostered a sense of community and history and created a comfortable atmosphere on the block. Karen Sander, executive director for the Downtown Boise Association, says that historic preservation is an important part of the city development and planning process "so that the fabric of the city is maintained ... our history gives us a sense of place." The CCDC's Sheldon adds that through the preservation of these buildings, memories and personal connections to downtown Boise are being saved. Sheldon says that while not all of Boise's historic downtown buildings are unique, the combination of buildings certainly is, and the variety should be preserved. Through historic preservation and mixed use, the corner of 8th and Idaho has become one of Boise's most prominent and popular spots. The block's streetscapes encourage pedestrian activity and promote outdoor enjoyment. Local historian J.M. Neill may have put it best when he said that people can sit at a table on 8th Street and feel like they are in San Francisco. "Not that we really want to imitate San Francisco, but having an occasional touch of San Francisco ain't too bad."

● ● ●

Jacey Brain graduated in December 2009 with a degree in history. A 2005 Capital High graduate, he will pursue a master's degree in U.S. history.

What are the most important aspects of a livable city?

"A great city is one that holds a sense of place. Cities are livable if their historical and natural aesthetics are acknowledged when looking to the future."

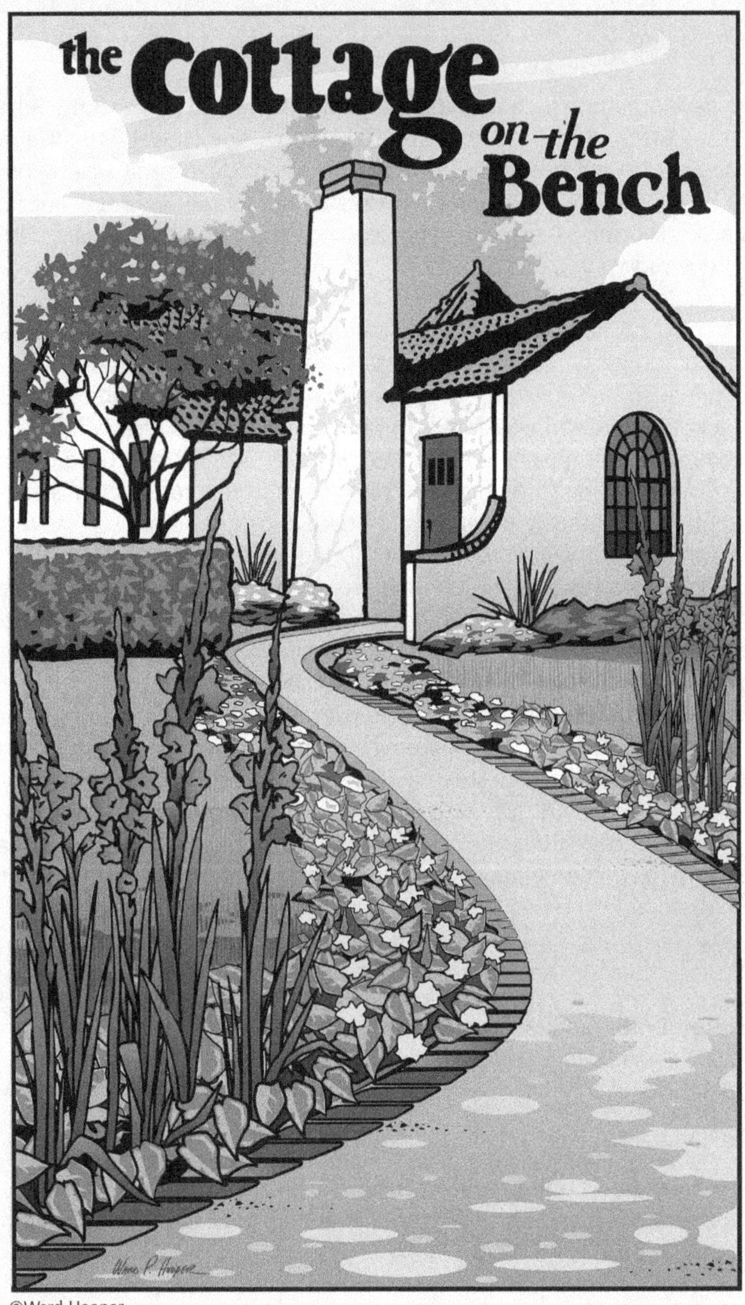

Artist Ward Hooper recalls the architecture of the 1920s in his tribute to the Boise Bench.

Revitalizing
THE BENCH

by Sarah M. Cunningham

oise's Central Bench neighborhood surrounding the Orchard Street corridor has been an area in decline, but under the right circumstances it has enormous potential to once again become a successful social space. What are the issues that face this long-established Boise neighborhood, one of the early suburbs that developed during the city's streetcar era? How can it be improved to restore its sense of community and rebuild its identity? There are no easy answers, but through a renewed sense of citizen involvement, the Central Bench can again stake its claim as one of Boise's thriving neighborhoods.

Historical relevance makes a profound contribution to the success of a social space—one that maintains a sense of its history while also serving the current needs and desires of the community. While there is little left to physically document the rich history of the Central Bench, the area can trace its roots back to the Oregon Trail and Boise's early settlement. The Bench was on the route of pioneering settlers who traveled the Oregon Trail as it followed the rim along Federal Way and westward on Overland to the lower valley near Emmett. Early in the 20th century, fueled by the new streetcar lines and canal system, the sagebrush-covered plateau quickly evolved into one of Boise's first suburbs. The construction of the canal system in the 1890s transformed the landscape from desert to fertile farms and orchards over much of the area between Boise and Meridian. The Boise River fed the main canals, which in turn supplied water to many smaller canals. People first began to settle the Central Bench area when the New York Canal was built in 1890. The local farmers favored the land southwest of the Boise River, believing the soil to be richer and more productive than that found in the lowlands. The arrival of the streetcar created an important and convenient connection to downtown industry and schools. After the streetcar ceased operating in 1928, the Bench lost a vital connection to the downtown. The automobile took over as the main mode of transportation and major traffic arterials began to cut through the neighborhood.

Until the early 1960s, the Bench area functioned as a community independent of the City of Boise. The sprawling neighborhoods were a strain to Boise officials, who made efforts to gradually incorporate them into the city. Robert Day, Boise's acting mayor in 1960, cited several reasons why he believed annexation would be beneficial to Boise, saying, "A growing demand for central government, and a growing demand for utilities has brought people to rely on the urban government ... the population is winning from two ends: they are able to use the city's resources without taxes and profit from the county's resources, which to a large extent are also paid by the people of Boise." The Bench was annexed into Boise shortly after these discussions in the early 1960s. Initially, Bench residents were vehemently opposed to annexation, arguing it would result in increased taxes. Later, residents recognized that enlarging the city limits would be beneficial to them because it would stabilize residential and commercial property values and encourage economic growth for an expanding population. In 1964, not long after annexation, the area became a focus in Boise's Comprehensive Plan. Under the plan, the Bench was to be "primarily residential" with "commercial uses along arterial streets" and "a system of neighborhood parks." The plan was updated in 1973 to allow higher-density residential areas and more commercial development.

As the area grew, traffic arterials overwhelmed and divided neighborhoods. Roadway and parking considerations took precedence over the quality of the social space and commercial development focused on the major streets, further increasing traffic and making the area less inviting to pedestrians. The success or failure of a street as a social space directly impacts the form, structure and comfort of the surrounding urban community. While the Orchard artery provides a thoroughfare for commuting traffic, it has created a sense of social isolation among commuters, neighborhood residents and businesses. Rather than continue as a dividing element in the community, Orchard has tremendous potential to become a "great street," one which urban designer Allan Jacobs describes as a social space that creates a sense of comfort and encourages participation in a community. "The interplay of human activity with the physical place has an enormous amount to do with the greatness of a street," he says. Successful streets and public spaces provide people with opportunities to gather, to be greeted and welcomed, and to be part of something larger than oneself, Jacobs explains.

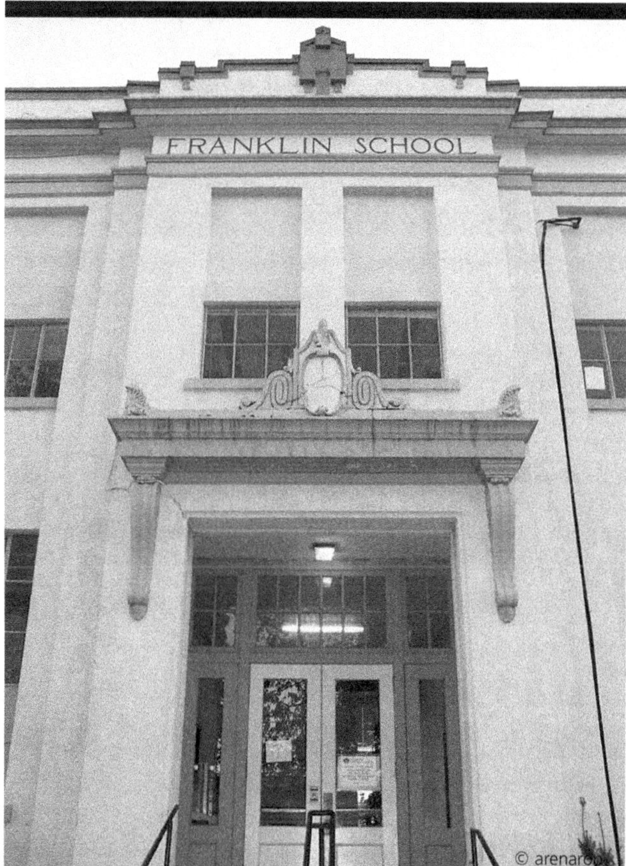

Residents have cited the 2009 demolition of Franklin School as a blow to neighborhood cohesiveness.

In keeping with the "great street" concept, redevelopment will need to focus on making the area more pedestrian and bicycle friendly. Infrastructure improvements, such as continuous sidewalks, more functional crosswalks and bike lanes and improved street lighting, should be priorities. Elaine Clegg, Boise City Councilwoman and special projects manager for Idaho Smart Growth, suggests one remedy might be to put the street on a "diet," an urban planning tactic used to slow traffic on busy thoroughfares by reducing

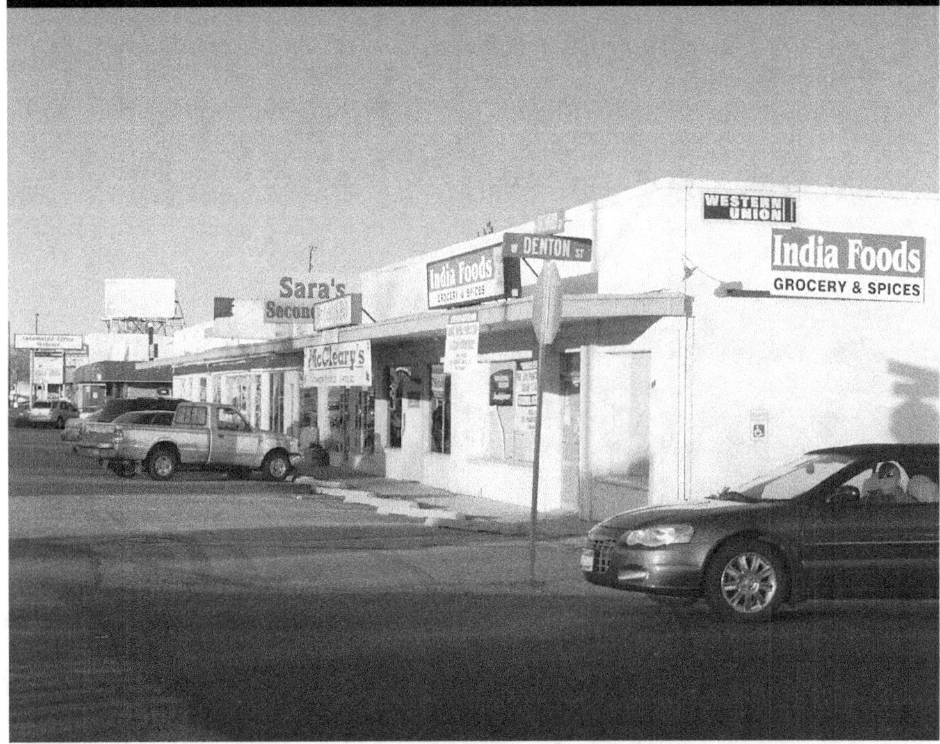

Ethnic markets suggest the growing immigrant and refugee population of the Central Bench. Pictured: the 600 block of North Orchard Street.

the number of lanes, thereby opening up space for safe and user-friendly sidewalks and bike lanes while making the social space of the community along the street much more inviting and interactive. Boise City Councilman David Eberle says years of disinvestment—a consequence of urban sprawl promoted by the false promise of lower costs of building outward rather than reinvesting in existing infrastructure and buildings—has contributed to decline on the Central Bench. This disinvestment manifests itself in the deterioration of some residential and commercial areas, and is evident in the poor maintenance of numerous strip malls along Orchard, a number of which are owned by absentee landlords. The 1960s-era mall at Emerald and Orchard provides an example. Beyond a vast desert of cracked asphalt and weeds, with a leaning light post and drooping electrical lines, the mall's exterior is seen by neighbors as an eyesore. The condition of the parking lot is the main cause of disappointment for business owners and neighboring homeowners alike. Recently, a few business owners attempted to reverse the appearance of neglect by paving a major portion of the parking lot. This, however, is more a band-aid than a successful remedy because the partial paving only adds to the mall's lack of cohesion. Despite their misgivings about the exterior appearance, residents are fond of the businesses within the mall, which offer great diversity to the community. Some tenants, including the Bosnian and Orient markets and the bowling alley, have made extensive interior renovations at their own expense to improve the ambiance of their businesses. If the owners could unite to collectively improve the entire exterior mall space as they have done with their individual interiors, the mall would increase its magnetism and become a successful social space.

The recent demolition of the historic Franklin Elementary School—closed permanently in June of 2008—has further degraded the community's cohesiveness. With the loss of the only Central Bench elementary school, students are bussed to schools outside their neighborhoods, compounding the loss of one of the oldest historical buildings on the Bench with a loss of neighborhood identity and involvement as children are spread to disparate locations outside their own neighborhood. Many residents mourn the demolition and loss of local history. While fearing the potential development of yet another strip mall or condensed housing units, the neighborhood remains hopeful that the property will be utilized for a park or some other purpose that contributes to the community. The school board has cleared the land and put it up for sale to pay for improvements made to other schools. If the board is sincere in preserving the health of the neighborhood where Franklin Elementary once existed, it will strive to find a conscientious buyer who will respect the interests of the residents. The Central Bench Neighborhood Association is working to rezone the property—now zoned as mixed-use—to exert more control over future uses. Whether it is a park or a venture with living units, social space and small businesses, the new development could be a positive addition to the Central Bench. If built for the neighborhood rather than as a destination for commuters, an appropriate use of the old school site could invigorate the neighborhood and bring new investment.

There is general agreement that the area is in decline and needs reinvestment. Councilman Eberle says the intersection of Orchard and Emerald is one of his favorite candidates for rehabilitation. Councilwoman Clegg has expressed a desire to see the Central Bench area redeveloped as well, saying that the City Council has had many projects on the list for the Bench but they have continued to fall down on the list of priorities. Councilman Alan Shealy acknowledges the city's focus in the downtown area and expressed the need to expand influence into other areas such as the Central Bench. Eberle says the new library at the Hillcrest Shopping Center has added an important service to the area, along with after-school programs at the elementary schools. But he feels commercial disinvestment along the Orchard corridor has to be resolved by the community. Clegg adds a similar sentiment, saying that she looks forward to seeing the community take action on its own behalf. Clegg and Eberle agree on the importance of a neighborhood association to voice concerns, access improvement funds and create cohesion. Both council members suggest the implementation of an Urban Renewal District to take advantage of tax-increment financing to fund reinvestment in the area. Small businesses along Orchard could unite to form an association and work together to create a cohesive commercial corridor. Eberle delights in the idea that Orchard could become an eclectic arts and culture hub of Boise similar to Portland's Hawthorne Street, with an identity created by the residents of the Bench community. Sustainable communities have been and can be redeveloped through these programs, and city officials agree that the endeavor will be more effective if the community participates in the redevelopment planning process.

One of the Central Bench's most important, yet understated, attributes is its cultural diversity. The neighborhood has a sizeable refugee and immigrant population, making it one of the more diverse areas in the city. Several businesses along the Orchard corridor reflect that diversity. For example, Oriental and Bosnian markets, along with Thai and Chinese restaurants, are all tenants at the mall on Orchard and Emerald. With its rich ethnic diversity, the neighborhood has the potential to become Boise's first International District, anchored by a Cultural Arts and Community Center that can celebrate the diversity that exists in the businesses already thriving in the area and give a social face to the diversity of the residents. Representatives from the refugee and immigrant population, as well as in the surrounding neighborhoods, say the center is something that Boise needs. Abu Mohammed, a new American from Somalia who lives on the Bench, says a cultural center could be a place where new Americans can feel welcome and receive assistance in finding jobs, in navigating the city and in understanding the cultural expectations of their new home.

Change, whether it means putting streets on a "diet," enhancing a strip mall, ensuring positive development at the Franklin School site or insti-

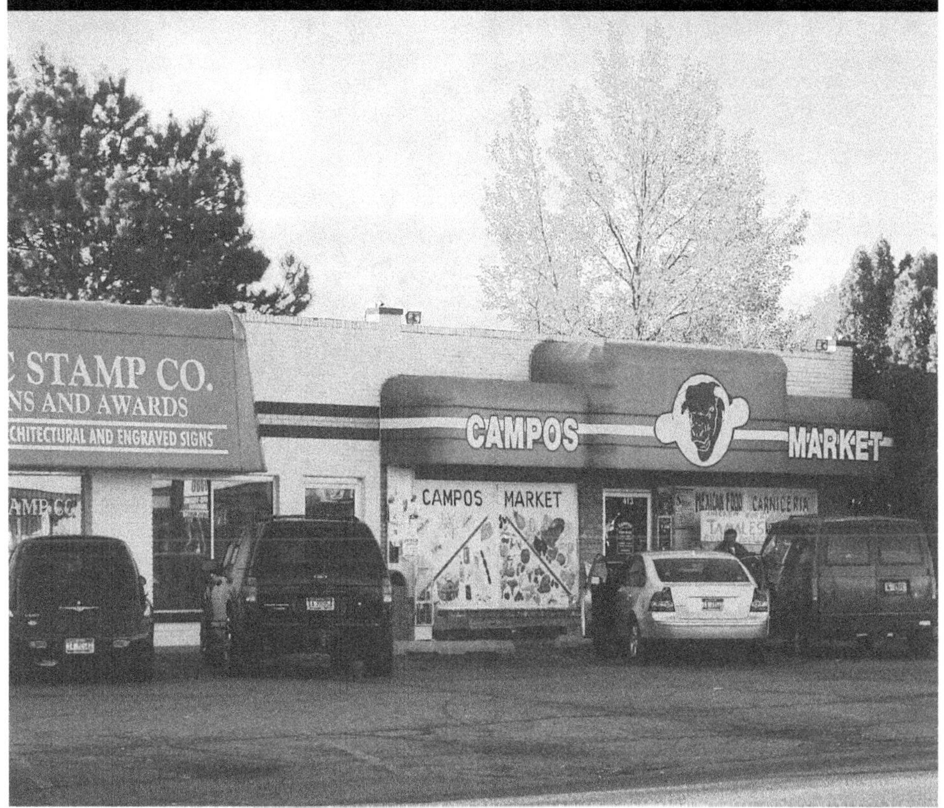

Immigrants from four continents—and from Somalia, Bosnia, Vietnam, Thailand, Mexico and many other places—are quietly remaking the Central Bench into an international district. Pictured: Campos Market on Orchard.

tuting an International District, will not come without citizen participation. The demolition of Franklin Elementary along with the distressed quality of the commercial thoroughfare, the lack of a satisfactory infrastructure for cyclists and pedestrians and rising crime rates inspired local residents last fall

A branch library in a vacant storefront contributes to the revitalization of the Hillcrest Plaza Shopping Center.

to reactivate the Central Bench Neighborhood Association to prevent the further disenfranchisement of their community. The CBNA is currently working to develop a comprehensive neighborhood plan to get the Central Bench community's input and expectations adopted in Boise City's Comprehensive Plan—Blueprint Boise. In recent meetings the CBNA emphasized neighborhood safety, community events and neighborliness as goals. The association has applied to the city for a neighborhood investment grant to assist in the development of a comprehensive neighborhood plan. The CBNA will sponsor several events this year, including its first Spring Celebration in Cassia Park to celebrate community, a neighborhood cleanup in June and a summer event organized in partnership with a neighborhood retirement center, aimed at bringing the community together. The association is also discussing preliminary steps to install Oregon Trail historic markers on Overland.

The current efforts to redevelop the disinvested areas of the Central Bench area seem to be driven by a quiet undercurrent of the City Beautiful movement of the early 20th century. History proves that if redevelopment of the area is motivated by civic pride, beauty and community, then the process of urban rebuilding will transform streets that are currently in decline into successful social spaces and "great streets." One important step is to acknowledge the disinvested social spaces in Central Bench area. "Civil courage in an ecological age means not only demanding social justice, but also aesthetic justice and the will to make judgments of taste, to stand for beauty in the public arena and speak out about it," wrote authors James Hillman and Michael Ventura. The decline of the commercial area is directly impacting the form, structure and comfort of the surrounding urban community. This can be overcome by grounding redevelopment endeavors in history, by building a sustainable community and by celebrating the diversity in the community. With the right public policies and neighborhood action, the Central Bench can again become a vibrant area with a sense of healthy community.

• • •

Sarah Cunningham graduated from Capital High School in 1991. She will earn a BA in general studies and a minor in leadership at the end of the fall 2010 semester. After graduation she plans to start two small businesses in the Bench area and later open an interdisciplinary design company.

What are most important aspects of a "livable" city?

"A livable city works to improve the overall quality and health of the environment to improve the quality of life for its citizens—streets, homes, waterways, air, soil and public buildings. It creates welcoming civic spaces for people to be social and interact with one another, experiencing being part of something larger than oneself"

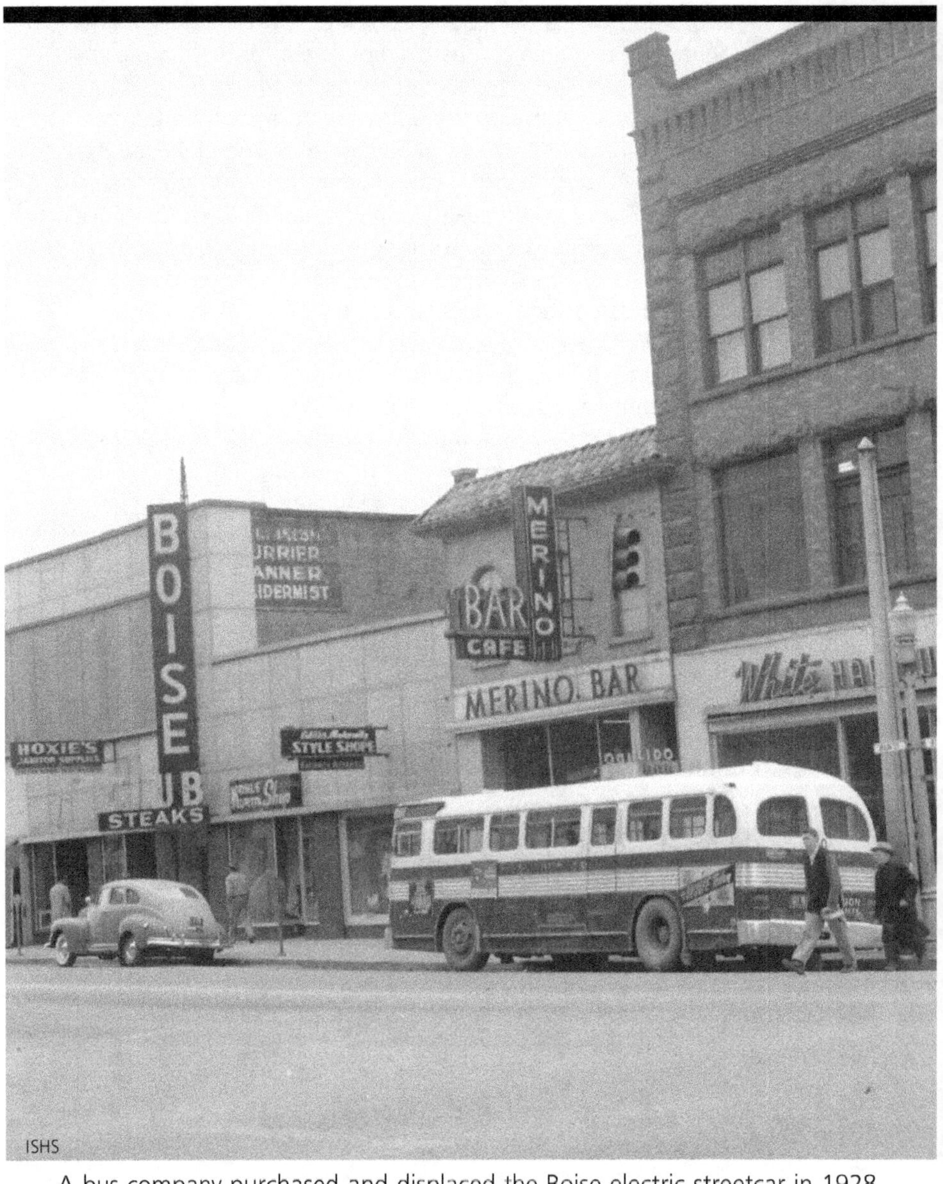

A bus company purchased and displaced the Boise electric streetcar in 1928. Pictured: buses on the 700 block of Main Street, about 1950.

Bus rapid TRANSIT

by Kelly Foster

magine a fleet of sleek buses moving swiftly in their own lanes on congested streets, passing lines of stop-and-go traffic as they deliver their regional passengers to a city's busy downtown core. That scene is unfamiliar to Boiseans, but not to commuters in similar-sized cities like Albany, NY; Eugene, OR and Santa Clara, CA, or in dozens of larger cities that have adopted what is known as "bus rapid transit" (BRT) systems to efficiently move thousands of commuters over crowded streets. What is now a vision in Boise will someday turn to reality. Planners are laying the foundation for what will be the city's first BRT route, which will run on State Street from downtown Boise to the intersection of State Street/State Highway 44 and State Highway 16 west of Eagle.

"Research study after research study has proven that expanding lanes for traffic doesn't solve congestion problems," says Kathleen Lacey, transportation planner for the City of Boise. "Dedicating seven lanes to auto traffic isn't going to solve the problem on State Street at all. We have a much better opportunity to solve it if we have bus lanes dedicated to transit only." With a myriad hurdles to jump—environmental impact statements, right-of-way acquisition, road expansion and infrastructure construction, to name a few—the rapid transit system may be several years away. However, should federal funds be received, the day the first specially-designed buses roll down State Street could occur within a fairly short time, says Lacey. Valley Regional Transit (VRT), the regional transit authority, in partnership with the Ada County Highway District (ACHD), is now leading the Traffic and Transit Operational Plan (TTOP). Consultants are currently studying traffic patterns, employment and residential growth projections and possible BRT routes. The finished TTOP report, due the fall of 2010, will determine how to integrate BRT into State Street's regular traffic flow and to outline the incremental steps needed to implement the system. With that report in hand, planning agencies will draft a master plan that will include land use scenarios along the corridor. Federal requirements must be met and right-of-way property purchased before the construction of bus lines and stations.

How long will all this take? Achieving BRT is a long-term effort, says Lacey. "We know people in the valley desire improved transit systems. We have so many steps to go through that it's not something we can manage in six years. It is going to take step-by-step, incremental improvements." But each improvement moves the region closer to achieving the transit vision. More than a million patrons rode the VRT system in 2009 and more frequent service is planned on State Street. Buses currently run every 30 minutes on the corridor. Within the year, VRT anticipates the buses will run every 20 minutes. And, of course, it is all a matter of money. The system will cost millions, and even with an infusion of federal funds, local governments will have to come up with a sizeable sum on their own. Implementation will be "very difficult" without local option taxing authority, says Lacey. A quarter cent increase in the local sales tax, for example, would be sufficient to fund a "high-quality" transit system for the entire valley, she says. The Idaho Legislature has been reluctant in the past to give local entities permission to levy local option taxes. So far, only cities in resort areas can utilize those taxes.

BRT is a new concept to Boise, but not new to transit systems. Cities throughout the world, from London, England to Cleveland, Ohio have selected BRT as a less expensive, but equally effective alternative to light rail or commuter rail transit. BRT is a mass transit system specifically designed for fast intercity/intercounty travel. It uses buses to provide transportation that is of a higher speed than ordinary bus routes or cars. To be effective, BRT needs special infrastructure so that bus systems can approach the quality of rail service, but at a lower cost. A BRT system is comparable to light rail in that both have stations at regular intervals, use dedicated lanes and travel at speeds faster than regular traffic. Like light rail, BRT also uses park and ride stations.

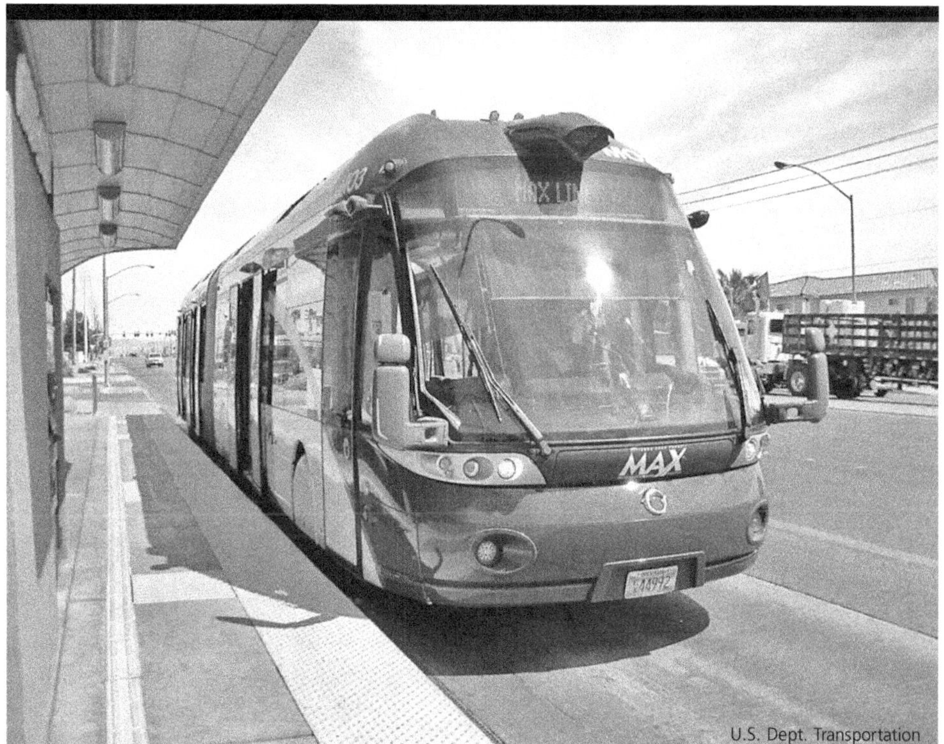

U.S. Dept. Transportation

The Federal Transit Authority promotes dedicated lanes with high-speed buses. Pictured: a MAX bus in Las Vegas, part of a BRT demonstration project.

One of the first infrastructure requirements is a main station where buses load and unload passengers, who can then walk to work or catch local buses or other modes of transportation. Boise is taking the first steps toward the construction of a multi-modal center in the heart of downtown. The current plan, which is subject to public hearings and City Council approval, calls

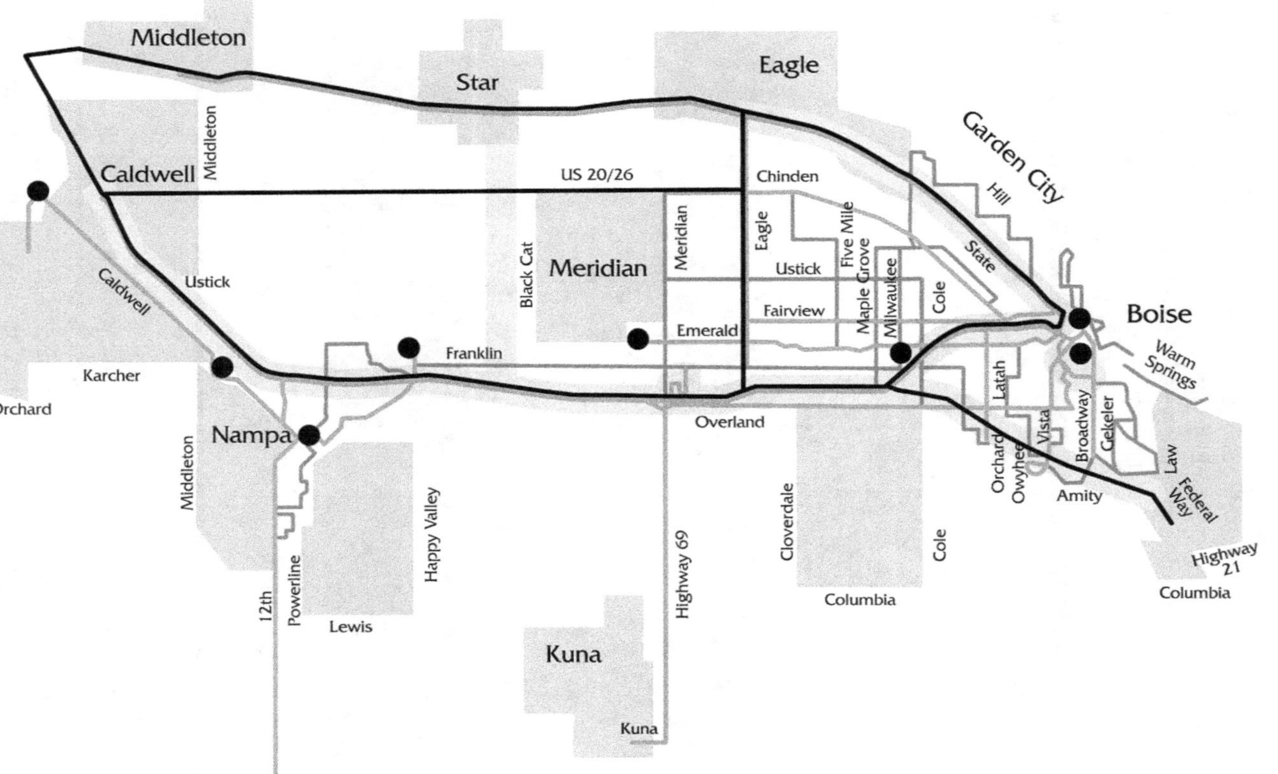

This map from Valley Regional Transit shows how high-speed buses would enhance service and increase ridership.

for a multi-level structure on the corner of 11th between Idaho and Bannock streets. The center will include 12 dedicated bus bays to serve both city and commuter bus systems and possibly a parking garage. Valley Regional Transit has $9 million set aside to buy property and construct the station.

Dedicated bus lanes are another vital BRT infrastructure requirement. The Boise area does not have any bus rights-of-way at the moment. Though ValleyRide, the Boise bus system operated to VRT, utilizes two dedicated bus lanes on four downtown blocks, these lanes are used solely for picking up and dropping off passengers. After loading riders, the buses must merge back into the normal flow of traffic. Like city buses, the Boise/Canyon County VRT shuttles use normal traffic lanes. To dedicate lanes for BRT means widening existing roads to accommodate those lanes or putting the roads on a "diet" by shrinking them by a lane on each side and dedicating those lanes to BRT. A Transit Priority System is also needed so stoplights along the BRT route are timed to give buses an early start through intersections. And transit stations and parking for passengers need to be built along the route. One important element for successful transit is what planners call "the last mile," generally assumed the longest distance that a passenger will walk between the station and work or home. People need to access the system safely and conveniently, explains Lacey, so planners will focus on pedestrian-friendly access and street crossings as well as lighting and other safety features.

While the system may be expensive at the outset, the financial picture has two sides. With BRT comes significant economic and social benefits—decreased air pollution, lower fuel consumption, reduced traffic and more efficient movement of people in and out of the city core. There is also an economic development side to BRT that has the potential to bring commercial and residential vitality to neighborhoods along the route. Along the State Street corridor, for example, planners are working to identify several areas for "transit-oriented development." These are 4-5 block "nodes" around future BRT stations where planners hope to attract high-density private development of offices, retail outlets, residential units and other services. The intent is to create a sense of place with open spaces, pedestrian- and bicycle-friendly access and mixed-use development, all conveniently clustered near a BRT station. "There is a demonstrated correlation between investment in transit stations and an increase in the economic value of the land adjacent to the station," explains Lacey. The TTOP study due this fall will recommend one site for early development as well as provide market data for up to 14 other potential locations along State Street and beyond. The State Street BRT project cuts across several jurisdictions and involves cooperation from a long list of parties—the cities of Boise, Garden City and Eagle, Ada County, the Ada County Highway District, the Idaho Department of Transportation, Valley Regional Transit and the Community Planning Association of Southwest Idaho (COMPASS). "Cooperation is absolutely essential for all

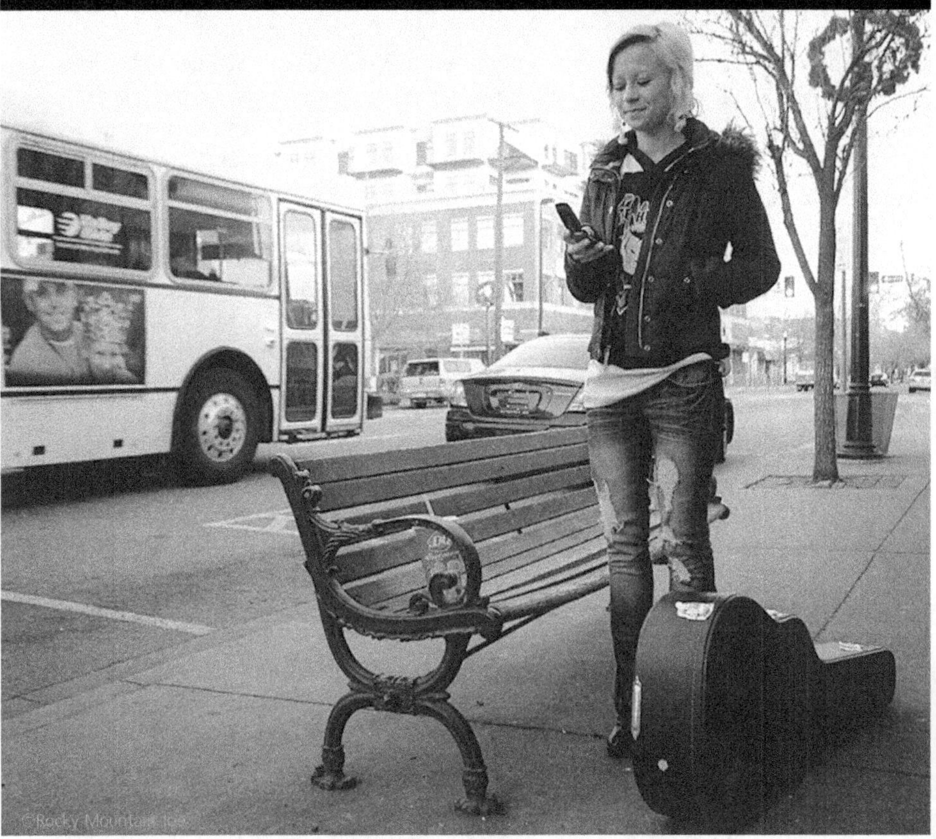

Intergovernmental cooperation is key to long-range planning for bus rapid transit. Pictured: a bus rider on Boise's Main Street.

those along the State Street corridor. This project cannot be done by just one jurisdiction because people are traveling so far between their employment and residence," says Lacey. "We have to understand each other's positions, funding circumstances and long-range planning efforts." While the State

Street corridor is Boise's first project dedicated to a long-awaited BRT transit system, there could be other places where the system will be implemented in the future. A valley-wide transit study is underway to determine ways to improve high-capacity transit. BRT could be a solution on east-west routes such as Fairview, Franklin or the rail corridor. Lacey says BRT typically requires a density of 12-14 residences per acre, ranging from single-family homes to high-density structures like apartments. Boise offers enough residential density to support BRT, but the Treasure Valley as a whole currently lacks the concentrated residential development required for a wider BRT network. So for now, the Treasure Valley will continue to use the Valley Regional Transit intercounty express system. That system has been in high demand ever since it started in 2000, and the buses are filled to capacity.

The City of Boise, COMPASS, VRT and many other entities understand the impact that a thriving public transit system can have on the economic and social life of the region. Several planning efforts have recently been completed or are currently underway to anticipate the valley's future transit needs and formulate a vision for the next generation of transportation projects—the Treasure Valley High Capacity Transit Study, Communities in Motion, Treasure Valley in Transit and the Downtown Boise Mobility Study. What all of these have in common is the understanding that the region needs a more efficient mass-transit system to move the increasing numbers of people who live in the valley. And in some ways, the future may resemble the past. BRT and the transit-oriented development concept is a throwback to the streetcar days of 100 years ago when stations stimulated developments such as Collister and Ustick. The past may not be prologue, but the streetcar era at least may be instructive as Boise tries to reduce traffic and as people reduce their dependence on the automobile. "It would be nostalgic and idealistic to say we are returning to a past era, but we have historical precedence that is applicable to the needs of today," says Lacey.

• • •

Kelly Foster, a 2007 Borah High graduate, is a junior art history major. After earning a BA degree, she plans to continue her studies with a focus on design.

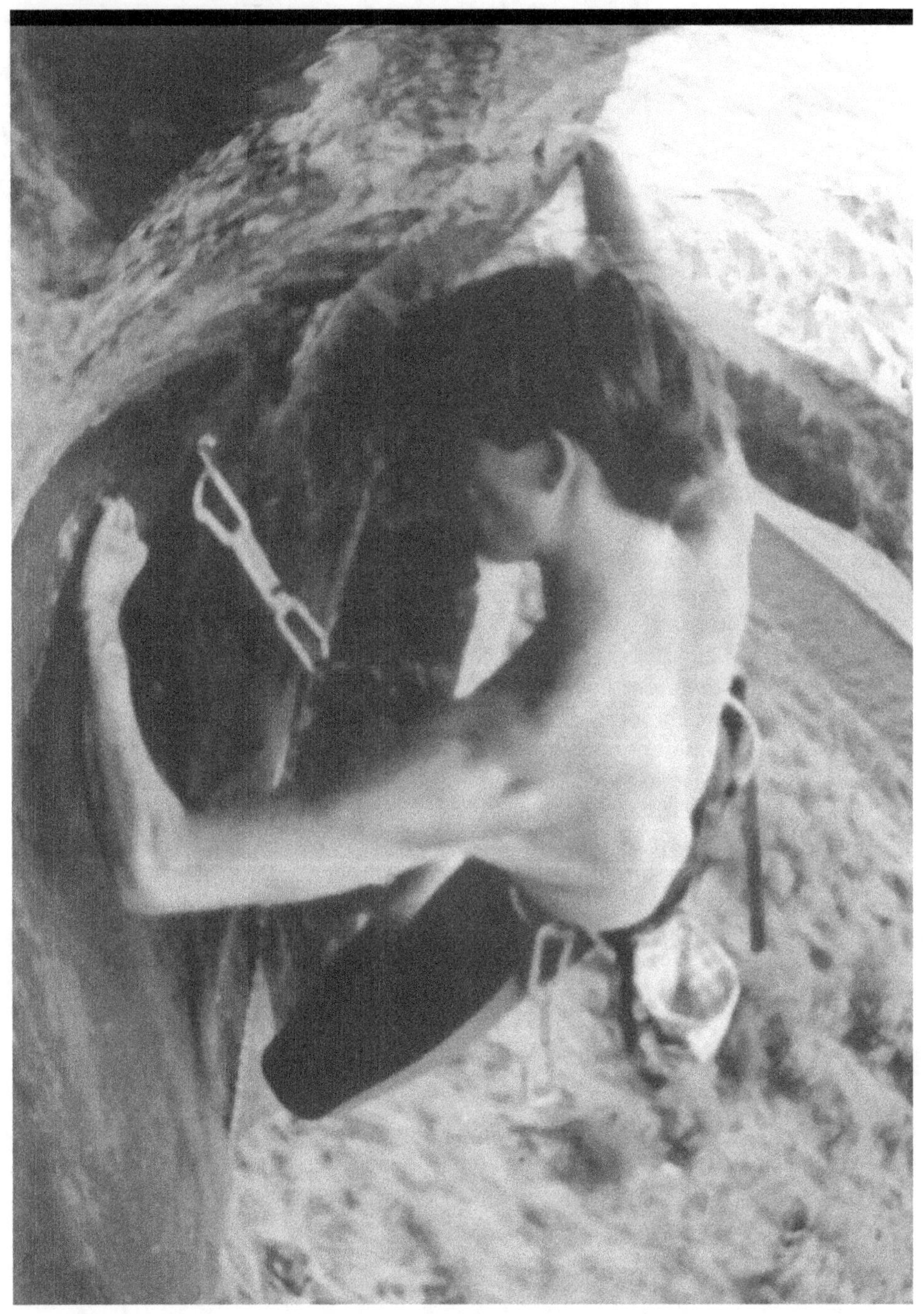

Author Tedd Thompson climbs the Black Cliffs below Hammer Flat, from the cover of a 1997 rock climber's guide.

Scaling

THE CLIFFS

by Tedd Thompson

From the calm of the place today, one would never know that only a few years ago the expanse of grass known as Hammer Flat was at the center of a spirited debate over Foothills development. The property located on a plateau north of Highway 21 between Diversion and Lucky Peak dams now enjoys quieter times, its tranquility only broken by the coming and going of wildlife. One day, however, the flora and fauna of Hammer Flat will be sharing their habitat when the placid plateau morphs into a planned community called The Cliffs. Approval for the development, named after the black basalt cliffs below the bluff, was granted by the Ada County Commission in December of 2006 amid concerns from Boise

---

Editor's note: The Boise City Council purchased Hammer Flat from Skyline Development as *Making Livable Places* went to press. While the controversy over The Cliffs is over, issues such as city-county jurisdiction and "sprawl" development remain.Tedd Thompson's case study of Hammer Flat can be instructive as similar projects come before city and county officials in the future.

residents, state wildlife officials and city hall. The proposal also sparked a jurisdictional tussle that focused on the city of Boise's influence, or lack thereof, over growth occurring outside its formal boundary.

The Hammer Flat saga began in 2005 after Boise-based Skyline Development Company purchased 707 acres next to the Boise River Wildlife

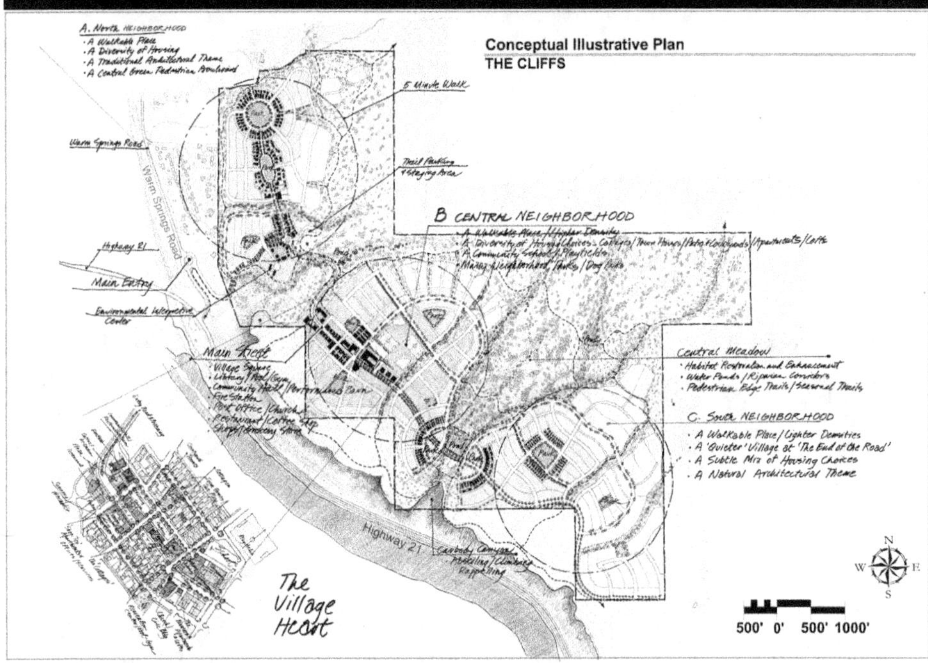

In 2005, Skyline Development Company purchased 707 acres for a planned community called The Cliffs. In March 2010, the Boise City Council voted to purchase the acreage for wildlife habitat.

Management Area, a 32,000-acre expanse in the Boise Foothills and Lucky Peak area set aside as prime habitat for deer and other wildlife. The intent, according to Skyline President Tucker Johnson, is to build a planned community, a land-use designation that implies a dense, urban-style development that will eventually become its own community of 3-4,000 people, complete with stores and other commercial enterprises, a school, fire station, parks and other services. At build out, The Cliffs will be a community of 3-4,000 people and include 1,350 homes, townhouses, cottages, businesses and parks on 350 acres. The other half of the property will remain open space, some of which will be dedicated to parks and sports fields. But most, approximately 270 acres adjacent to the Boise River Wildlife Management Area, will be set aside as natural open space that will feature restored habitat for deer, elk and other animals. Skyline's first step was to seek approval from Ada County, including a zoning change from rural preservation, which allowed one house per 40 acres, to a higher density required by a planned community. As The Cliffs plan began to work its way through the county's approval process, it drew strong reactions from a variety of sources and for a variety of reasons. To those opposed, The Cliffs was a poorly conceived, partially planned development that would consume prime Foothills wildlife habitat, conflict with the city's Foothills Management Plan, increase Boise traffic and burden city taxpayers. To supporters, The Cliffs was a well-planned community that would provide homes and other amenities for people who love nature and want to live in a wildlife-friendly area. And to decision-makers, The Cliffs represented the classic political balancing act, with private property rights on one hand and the city's strong open spaces ethic on the other.

Among the concerns expressed, one seemed to receive the most emphasis: the potential impact on wildlife, including a loss of habitat for the deer and elk herds that winter graze on the plateau. In a cover letter to his "Hammer Flat Development" report, Al Van Vooren, the Idaho Department of Fish and Game's Southwest Regional Supervisor at the time, offered an opinion that spoke to many citizens' concerns about The Cliffs' shortcomings: "Simply not building on part of the land does not mitigate or compensate for building on the rest of the property." Skyline, says Johnson, has addressed the environmental concerns through a mitigation plan that he says will improve the habitat on the plateau to make it even friendlier to wildlife. The natural open space portion will be closed forever to development. Original species of foliage will be planted and the land will be closed to all foot, bike and motorized traffic in the winter months. Johnson said that a portion of all real estate transactions will go into a fund dedicated to restoring the natural habitat. "We will replant bitterbrush, sagebrush and grasses that are native to the area. These are the foods the wildlife originally ate—not cheat grass and cattle feed." Recycled wastewater may be used to water the native plants. Reintroducing some of the original plant species also will reduce fire risk, he added. The mitigation plan, which will guide Skyline's use of the undeveloped portion of the project, was approved when the Ada County Commission gave the green light to the development. "We recognize that there are antelope and deer in this location," says Ada County Commissioner Fred Tilman. "But there are ways we can mitigate the impacts of having another use on the property. At the end of the day, we were convinced that the mitigation plan was adequate to resolve the concerns."

Prior to Skyline's application to the county, Boise's Mayor Dave Bieter went clearly on record as opposing the development. As Bieter expressed in a letter to the Ada County Commissioners on Jan. 13, 2005, "High density residential development of Foothills properties immediately adjacent to the Wildlife Management Area will, on a year round basis, bring people, pets, motor vehicles, noise, light and general activity that will be harmful to the area's sensitive habitat resources." Bieter stated other issues that will directly affect Boise: "The Hammer Flat property appears inappropriate for a high density development. This is especially true if it does little more than accommodate residential home sites that create a disproportionate burden on City infrastructure and public lands in the Boise Foothills." Bieter's concerns led to a policy question: How much influence does the city have on development outside its boundary? The answer: Not as much as it would like.

Each city in Ada County has an "area of impact," which is a negotiated boundary around the city where planners feel future development and eventual annexation might occur. A city's area of impact is still under the jurisdiction of the county, but when a development is proposed, the county often consults with the city over such issues as building codes and zoning laws. The Boise City Council reviews applications for development in the area of impact just like it does for those in the city limits and then forwards its concerns to the county, says Michael Zuzel, assistant to Mayor Bieter. "The county is free to take our advice or not," he says. Zuzel adds that there is considerable communication between the city and county at the staff level when development is proposed within the area of impact. Commissioner Tilman says the county respects the concerns of the city. "We always ask for comment and try to look at the information that is made available," he says.

But for land outside the area of impact, such as The Cliffs, decision-making is solely in the hands of the county. Even though the city registered its concerns about The Cliffs, the county had jurisdiction over land contiguous to Boise's area of impact. "The city's main concern was wildlife habitat," says Zuzel. "The development was close enough to the city limits that even though it wasn't in the current area of impact, eventually it could become a part of the city. So the mayor and council felt an obligation to weight in on that." Mayor Bieter, quoted in an Aug. 14, 2005, *Idaho Statesman* report, said, "It's no secret that pressure to urbanize the area east of Boise has grown tremendously. The geography of the area virtually assures that the City of Boise will sooner or later be the one to provide services there and we've already done planning in that area as part of the Foothills open space effort." Given the city's concerns over the potential impacts of The Cliffs, the City Council came up with a means to exert more influence on the decision—expand Boise's area of impact to include the development. "By including it in the area of impact at least that would bring us into the discussion," explains

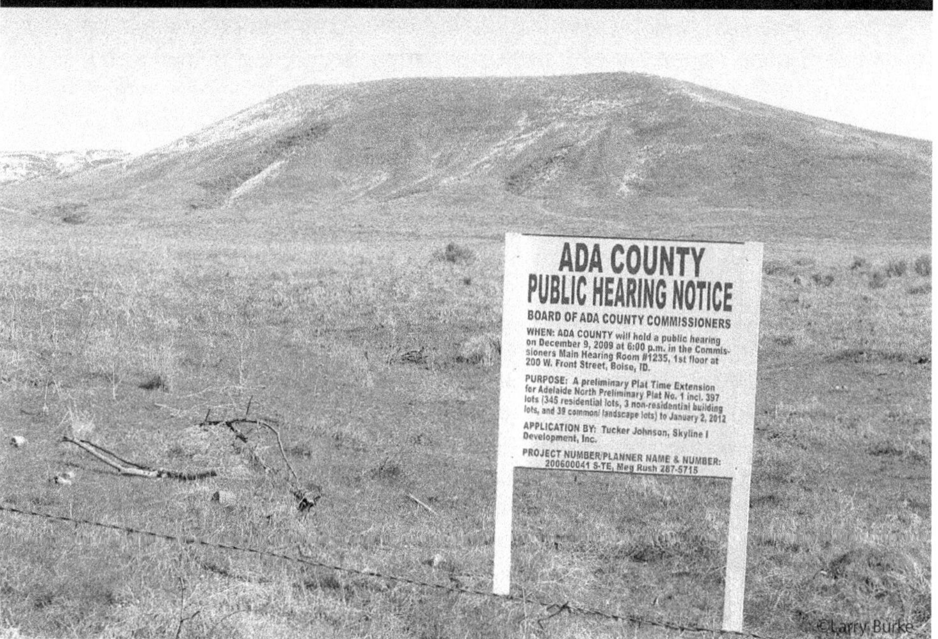

Notices for public hearings were frequent sights in the Foothills when the development of Hammer Flat was under consideration by the Ada County Commission.

Zuzel. The City Council approved the concept on Feb. 22, 2006, but before the city and country could negotiate new impact boundaries, Skyline filed an application to build The Cliffs, which meant the project would fall under the existing area of impact. Skyline later filed a petition for judicial review in Fourth District Court to challenge the city's efforts to expand the area of impact, claiming there were legal, factual and procedural flaws in the city's proceedings. With Skyline's application moving forward, the area of impact expansion became a moot point—the decision to approve or reject The Cliffs remained wholly in the county's hands.

As Skyline's proposal worked its way through the county's approval process, the opposition and developer presented their respective cases to local officials and in the media. Save the Plateau, a group organized by engineer and Hammer Flat resident Anthony Jones, presented more than 3,000 postcards, e-mails, Web comments and petition signatures calling for protection of the area. And 110 of the 130 who testified at hearings were in opposition. Skyline responded with newspaper advertising, guest opinions and testimony rebutting claims and explaining the benefits of the new community. The county's Planning and Zoning Commission approved the project by a 4-3 vote. After another round of testimony two months later, all three county commissioners then approved The Cliffs on Dec. 20, 2006. As with all new development, the county commissioners weighed the opinions of the city and the affected neighbors, evaluated how an additional community could affect air pollution, traffic, fire and police, and then determined if the builder's plan met state law and county ordinances. "It is important to realize what our job is in these types of hearings," says Tilman. "We are a quasi-judicial body ... we are there to listen to the facts, not emotions, and apply the law and our ordinances. We describe what the facts are and apply that to what the law is."

But opposition continued. Save the Plateau leaders turned to the courts a year later, filing a petition in Fourth District Court to determine if the county's action complied with federal, state and county laws. Another year went by before the Judge D. Duff McKee ruled in favor of Ada County, saying allegations against the commissioners were "without merit." "If we had taken our personal views and not evaluated the development based on the facts, then I believe Skyline would have cause for an action that we were denying them the use of their property... the land-use laws focus on private property rights," says Tilman. "We have to consider, what does the law say? What do ordinances say? Did we give all parties due process in implementing the law? Was our decision based on the facts? Did they comply with the laws and ordinances? Those are the real questions," he adds.

The Cliffs was approved with a development agreement that specified 75 conditions of approval that must be met before building permits can be issued. "We both agree that the applicant will fulfill certain conditions. If the developer fails to meet them, they can't develop ... approval is withdrawn. It is a step-by-step process—if you miss a step, the process is done," says Tilman. Many of the conditions won't come into play until construction begins, Johnson says. Then, standards for drainage, roads, soils and lot dimensions must be satisfied. Skyline also has worked out agreements regarding library services and schools, and will build a new fire station and wastewater plant once construction begins. Skyline is on track to meet those conditions, but one vexing issue remains—access to the property.

The company's original plans included a roundabout main entrance off Highway 21 approximately 1,000 feet north of the Warm Springs and Idaho

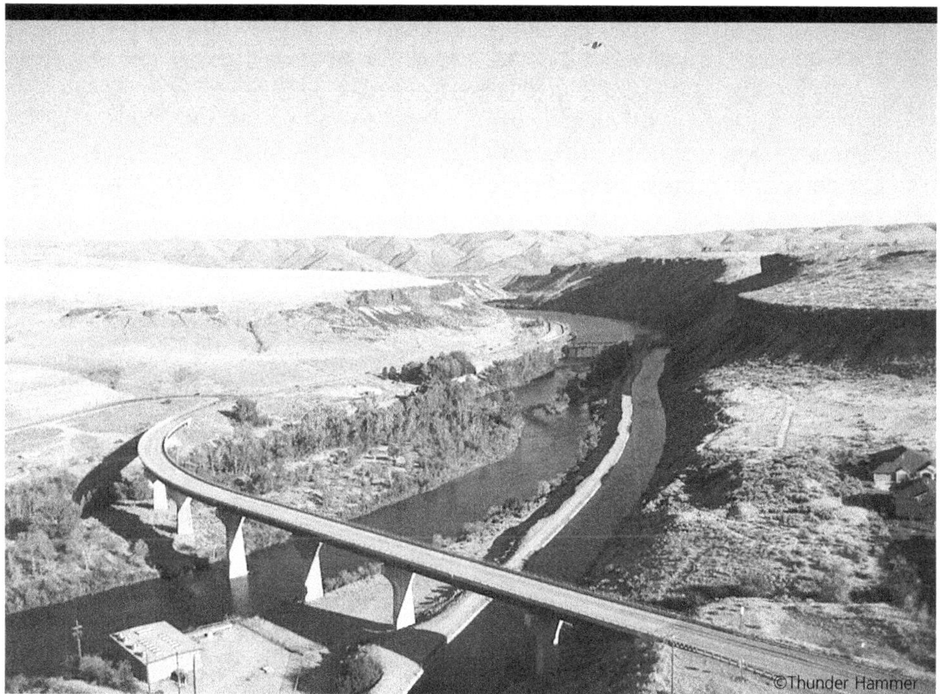

Access to Hammer Flat (bluff at center-left of photo) was not resolved prior to the property's sale to the City of Boise.

21 intersection. But the development company doesn't own any land that fronts Highway 21. The piece of property that Skyline originally thought it could use is owned by the Idaho Transportation Department, which plans to keep the land for a future traffic interchange, according to Pam Golden, Development and Access Management Engineer for ITD. "Without question, that is one of the key issues," says Johnson. "If we don't change their mind, the project has a challenge." Johnson adds that there is limited access on the western end of the property that could serve as an alternative road for the first phase of the development. But it doesn't have the capacity to serve the entire community.

One obstacle not on the radar screen in 2005 is another major reason the development hasn't started—the slow economy. That has put The Cliffs in a holding pattern, waiting for the market to turn and lenders to loosen the purse strings. "The magnitude of the market collapse has certainly frozen things," says Johnson. "There is no demand; fortunately, we did not have a lot of infrastructure in. But our application application did have six zeros behind it." Skyline has been in business for more than 40 years and has seen real estate ups and downs like this before. "My father, Ted Johnson, started this business in 1967. We have been developing in the Boise area ever since. We noticed that about every five to seven years there is a slowdown in the market. We are always subject to the forces of the market ... we knew this correction was overdue; we just didn't expect that it would drop in its value so enormously." Johnson says his company bought Hammer Flat in the middle of the building boom, but might have done so no matter what the current economy was. "When the land went up for sale we heard that some buyers from out of town were interested. We saw Hammer Flat as a perfect opportunity to build something that would be good for Boise," says Johnson. "I have 10 brothers and sisters; nine of us live in the valley. It is important to us that we have a great place for our children and grandchildren to live. We hope that The Cliffs will be a model for good development in the future." It may be some time before Johnson's hope can be borne out. First, the market has to turn around. "It is tough to predict the future when the pattern has been interrupted," he says. But even if it takes another year or year and a half before they start, he expects it will be 2020 before the development is "built out."

The saga of The Cliffs' approval may be over, but what about the next development? Will Boise's voice be heard? Zuzel says Ada County and its cities are working on the area of impact issue through the cooperative planning effort called Blueprint for Good Growth. Blueprint "calls for a more dependable process for setting boundaries," Zuzel says. He adds that planners are looking more into the future—a 20-year window instead of the usual 10—which means in many cases area of impact boundaries will be drawn further away from cities than they are now. "One idea of Blueprint is to channel urban development into urban areas. In theory, we wouldn't have many situations where there is an urban style development outside anybody's area of impact," says Zuzel. The city's primary concern is to limit "sprawl" development, he adds. "this mayor and council are resolute in their conviction that if you channel development into urban areas—areas that are already developed or that can be developed more—that is a better deal environmentally and a better deal financially. The capacity is already there. You don't have to spend more dollars to support that development. That's a better deal for the taxpayers," Zuzel says. Zoning laws, explains Tilman, create a "gray area" in the planning process because a city may zone property one way and the county another, which can cause problems when the properties are contiguous. Says Tilman: "This especially comes into play regarding density. That's why we have some differences with cities over planned communities. Those are an urban density, like a small city. Cities are saying, 'Wait a minute ... you shouldn't be planning that in a rural area and that it should be connected to the city. We want to determine how it should be planned even though it is in the county.'"

A house that sits above a scenic river with views of snow-capped mountains, with elk, deer and antelope nearby, with access to hiking, biking and climbing just outside the front door and downtown only minutes away, may seem like a dream—the type of dream that draws people to Idaho. As developments like The Cliffs turn this dream into reality, many wonder at what price. Although Skyline has been conscious of wildlife concerns and followed all the rules of the county and state, many still oppose the development of Hammer Flat. Opponents to The Cliffs, whose protests did not carry the day with the Ada County Commission, might feel that development will continue and that's that. While change might not take place in the exact way or at the exact time a person wants, the public's opinion does matter. The rules that are in place for the next development to come along will be standards set by builders, planners, commissions and lawmakers who have learned something from the past. Citizens must educate themselves and then speak up if they want change to follow a certain direction. Change is inevitable, but how we change isn't.

· · ·

Tedd Thompson, a 1981 Borah High graduate, is a junior majoring in art history. After graduation he plans a trip to Europe to "see what they are doing right and what we might do better."

What are the most important aspects of a "livable" city?

"I grew up climbing on the Black Cliffs and Table Rock. The thing that has kept me around Boise, and hopefully will always keep me around Boise, is the easy access to open spaces. Being able to climb, mountain bike and fish without traveling is essential to livability for me. If we as a community recognize the importance of our open space, Boise will continue to be a great place to call home."

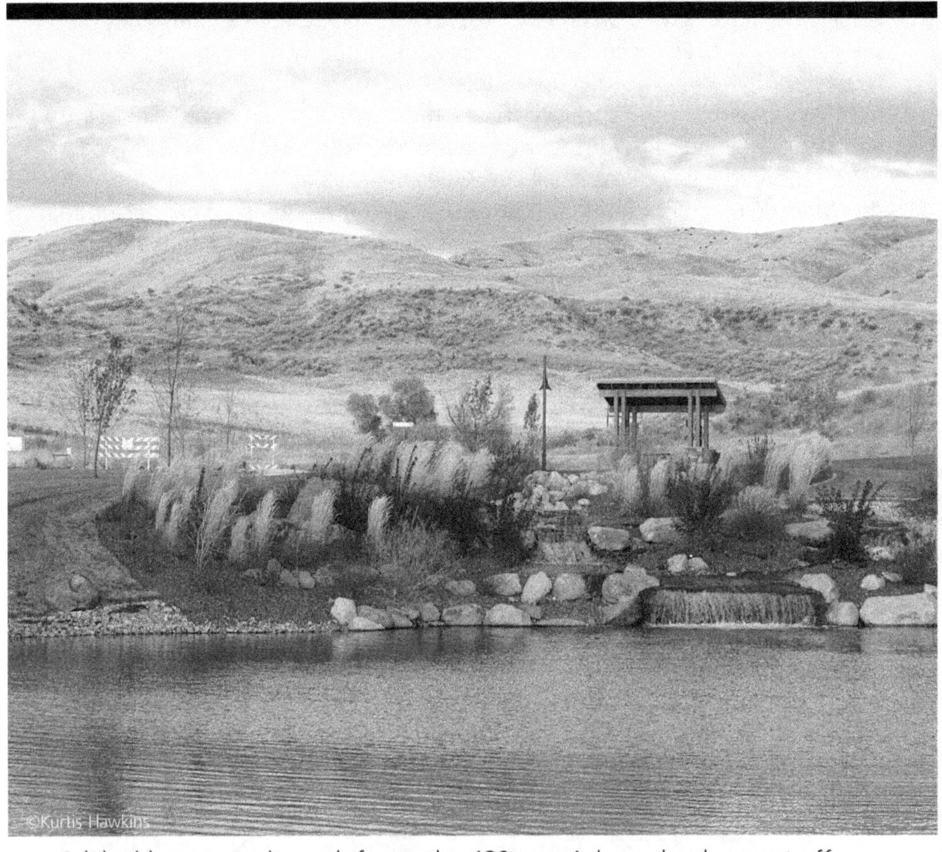

A lakeside community park fronts the 480-acre Avimor development off Highway 55.

More like
AVIMOR?

by Kurtis Hawkins

The Avimor planned development has been a major source of controversy since its land purchase in July of 2003. Questions about sustainability, wildlife impact, foothills conservation, traffic influx and
other issues are significant to the valley because Avimor proposes to
eventually build 12,000 new homes. The property encompasses 23,000 acres
in the area off Highway 55 between Boise and Horseshoe Bend. The first
platted village now under development is approximately 480 acres. Other villages are on the drawing board. Avimor is one of the first planned communities to exist in the foothills region northwest of Boise, and as such, can be a
case study for future developments that will surely follow.

A planned community like Avimor is a designed grouping of varied and
compatible land uses, such as housing, recreation, commercial centers and
industrial parks, all within one contained development. To put it more simply,
a planned community is zoned for mixed-use. Unlike typical subdivisions that

are zoned only for residential and recreational parks, Avimor eventually will host a variety of uses ranging from housing to commercial retailers.

Spanning three different counties and existing several miles from any city, Avimor and the issues surrounding its development are complex and controversial. For starters, every city has a boundary, and directly outside of that is what is known as the city's area of impact. Because of close proximity, many factors can affect a city from within its area of impact, such as traffic influx, landfill usage, infrastructure development, emergency service capability and many others. Avimor sits immediately outside of Boise's legal area of impact but, as Mayor David Bieter believes, it still will have a great effect on Boise's services and infrastructure. Because the development is on land governed by Ada County, the decision to approve Avimor was made by the county commissioners. Throughout the process several concerns were expressed about the potential impact on Boise and the area surrounding Avimor. New Urbanists and environmentalists resist developments that encourage commuters to drive long distances to and from work. Some citizens and wildlife experts also weren't sure what the impact would be on large game. This is a concern because Avimor is being built on a critical wintering range for a variety of animals like deer and elk. Developments like Avimor can push wildlife into less habitable locations because of noise, pets and fenced-off areas. Even though Avimor has an extensive wildlife mitigation plan, it is impossible to know exactly what effect it will have on the existing wildlife.

In 2006, when Avimor received approval from Ada County, Boise filed a petition for judicial review in Fourth District Court questioning the substance and procedures of the county's decision. An article in the *Idaho Statesman* explains Boise's reason for filing the appeal, stating, "The commissioners appeared to have made up their minds in advance, violating their roles as independent reviewers and decision-makers." Mayor Bieter stated his concerns in a different *Statesman* interview: "While Avimor is technically outside the City of Boise's area of impact, it will have a direct effect on our services and infrastructure," meaning the majority of people living in Avimor will commute to and work in Boise. He believes that increased traffic on already-congested State Street will decrease air quality and impact downtown parking—and that these commuters will not be paying Boise City property tax, even though they will surely be using some of Boise's services. After Boise filed its appeal against Ada County, the City of Star filed as an *amicus curiae*, or "friend of the court." Star's case stated that in attempting to interfere with the land-use decisions of another jurisdiction, Boise threatens the authority of Star and other cities that have a stake in the Avimor development and others like it. As it turned out, Judge D. Duff McKee dismissed Boise's appeal, saying the city had no standing in court. Ada County's decision to allow Avimor stood. What can Boise do to prevent future developments from impacting the city in this way? Michael Zuzel, Mayor Bieter's assistant, explained that as far as these "leapfrog" developments are con-

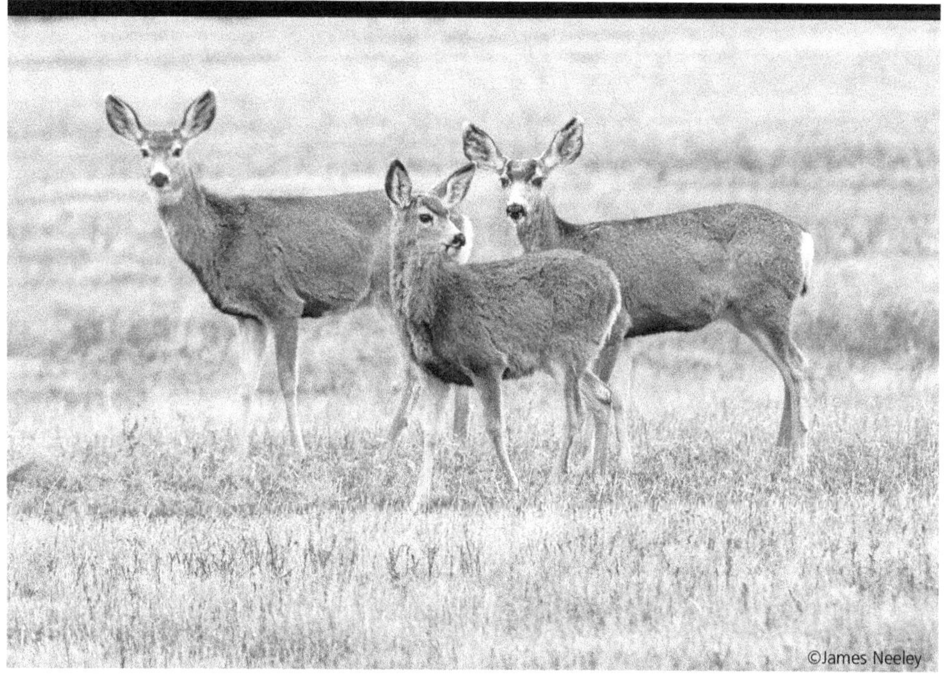

Mule deer in the Boise foothills. Avimor has promoted "zero net loss" of wildlife habitat. Critics say the development contributes to sprawl.

cerned, there is really nothing the city can do. If a development is under the county's jurisdiction, the city has no say over it. It is more difficult for a planned development to get permits than it is for small developments like subdivisions. There are many stipulations that result when a development classifies itself as a planned community. They must be at least 640 acres and be self-contained, meaning they provide for infrastructure like roads, water, electrical power and wastewater treatment. Ada County approved Avimor after developers met the required codes and ordinances and satisfied the conditions put on the project before it could begin.

Eventually, Avimor's three phases of development will cross through Ada, Gem and Boise counties. The amount of traffic added to State Highway 55 is being studied by the Idaho Transportation Department. ITD and Avimor are working to develop a way to enhance the current highway access and

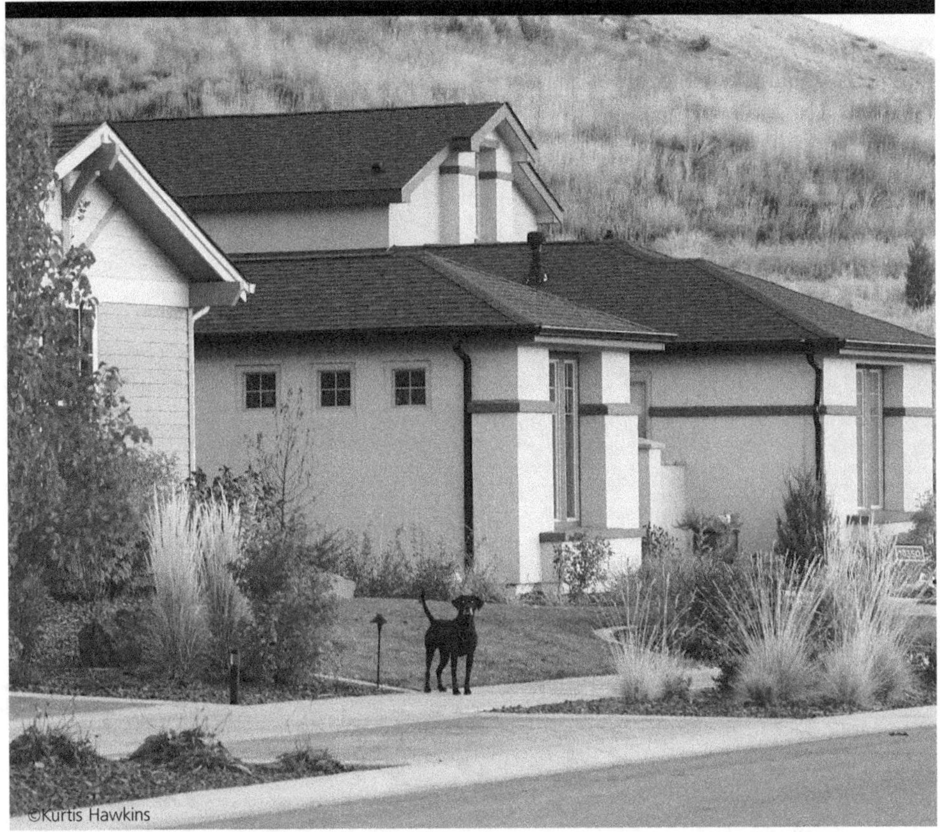

Avimor is for sale by SunCor, the original developer. Twenty-three homes have been sold in the project's first two years.

better suit it for the inevitable increase in traffic. The environmental impact of Avimor is a concern that the developers have addressed with a comprehensive wildlife mitigation plan. Developed by Charles Baun of Boise-based Environmental Conservation Services, Inc., the plan explains how Avimor will attempt to limit its impact on the environment. Avimor will withhold 70 percent of its property as open space and will institute a "zero-net-loss" policy designed to improve substandard land and prevent the displacement of wildlife. The land is surveyed and rated on a one through ten scale. A rating of "one" represents land that is unfit for wildlife habitat; the rating of "ten" represents land that is completely rife with plant and animal life. Overall, the report rates the land at an average of "four." Most of the land is cheat grass that does not sustain much animal life and provides ready fuel for wildfires, says Baun in the plan. Every time a house is sold, the seller pays .5 percent of the gross sales price to the Avimor Stewardship Organization. Those funds will be used to restore vegetation on lower-rated, substandard land so the rating can go from, for example, a "four" to an "eight." By improving the quality of open space, Avimor makes up for the land that houses consume and creates a zero-net-loss of land. The mitigation plan also defines areas that are crucial for wintering animals and explains how these areas will not be fenced, which will prevent wildlife from migrating to other less sustaining areas. Avimor is also trying to reduce its carbon footprint through the building standards it uses. *The Idaho Statesman* published a story about the advantages of building "Energy Star" rated homes, stating, "During 2008, SunCor Idaho Inc. built 19 Energy Star-certified homes in Avimor. These 19 homes are equivalent to eliminating the emissions from nine vehicles and planting 15 acres of trees."

The development is for sale as SunCor's parent company, Pinnacle West, restructures its business. In March 2010, five of Avimor's six staff members were laid off and sales were halted pending the sale of SunCor's assets, according to the *Idaho Statesman*. There are currently 23 houses at Avimor—20 occupied and three that have been sold but that Avimor is leasing back from the buyers. Most of the occupants moved in last summer. The last closing occurred in December 2009, and no houses are under construction at the current time. Avimor has not been spared from the harsh real estate market forces that are affecting other developers. "The economic impact has been profoundly difficult," says John Rogers, sales manager for Avimor. "Housing may have cratered deeper than other sectors, but nobody's getting a free ride on this roller-coaster. Ultimately, the impact has been two-fold—first, to brutally separate the wheat from the chaff, both on an individual developer level and on a development model level, and second, to galvanize the public into re-evaluating their reasons to buy."

Planned communities like Avimor, he says, are better prepared to weather the economic storm. Most are well-funded endeavors with long timeline horizons that can survive market cycles. Avimor, for example, is a 30-year project. "Quality of life issues are of paramount concern for the planned-community developer. If he wants the product to be attractive and

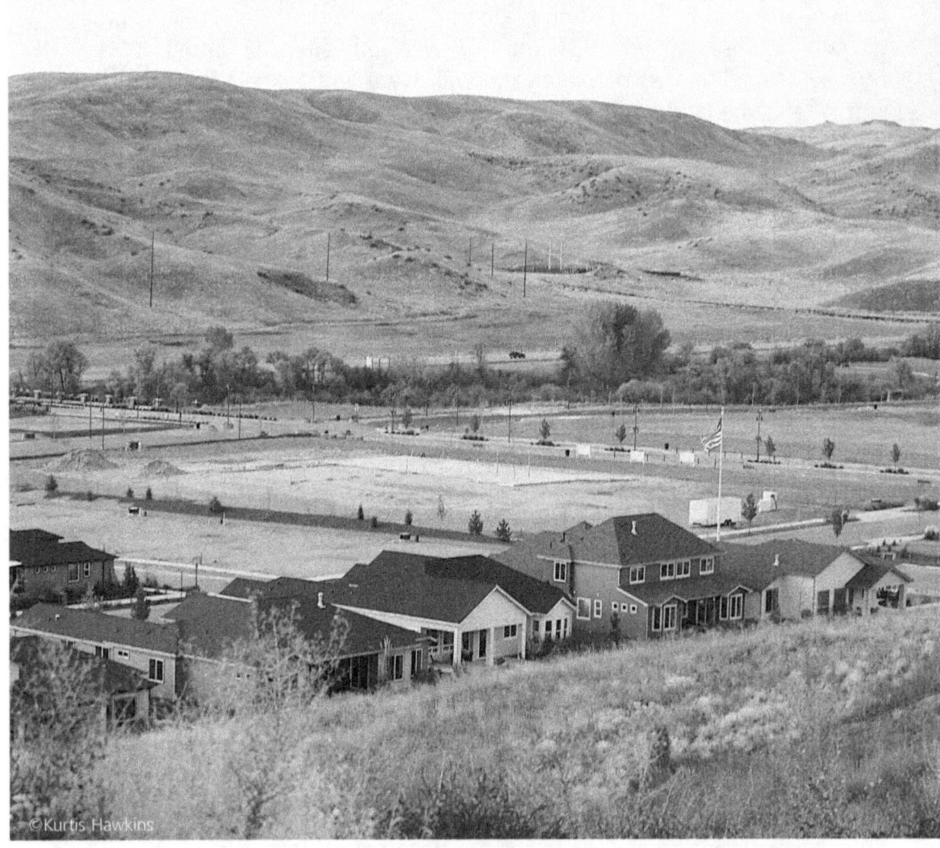

Large planned communities such as Avimor may be the future of foothills development in Ada County. Pictured: Avimor, slowed by the recession in the fall of 2009.

profitable 25-30 years hence, he cannot undermine the quality of life of his previous residents by his own efforts or lack of foresight. The master-planned community is the model of the future and the reasons are obvious," says Rogers. Avimor may have been one of the valley's the first, but it won't be the last planned community. Prior to the nation's economic slowdown, a dozen or more planned communities were in Ada County's application process. That number has dropped by half due to the economy. Even at that, it is evident that the planned community mode of development will play a role in the region's future. Understanding the ways that people view developments like these and being knowledgeable about the process to approve and govern them is important in keeping the Boise area sustainable for many years to come.

• • •

Kurtis Hawkins is a 1999 graduate of Payette High School. He will receive his BA in mass communication in spring 2010. He plans to begin work next winter on a master's degree in the philosophy of communication, with the goal of teaching at the college level.

What are the most important aspects of a "livable" city?

"A positive, shared understanding of what a city is and should be will make any city livable."

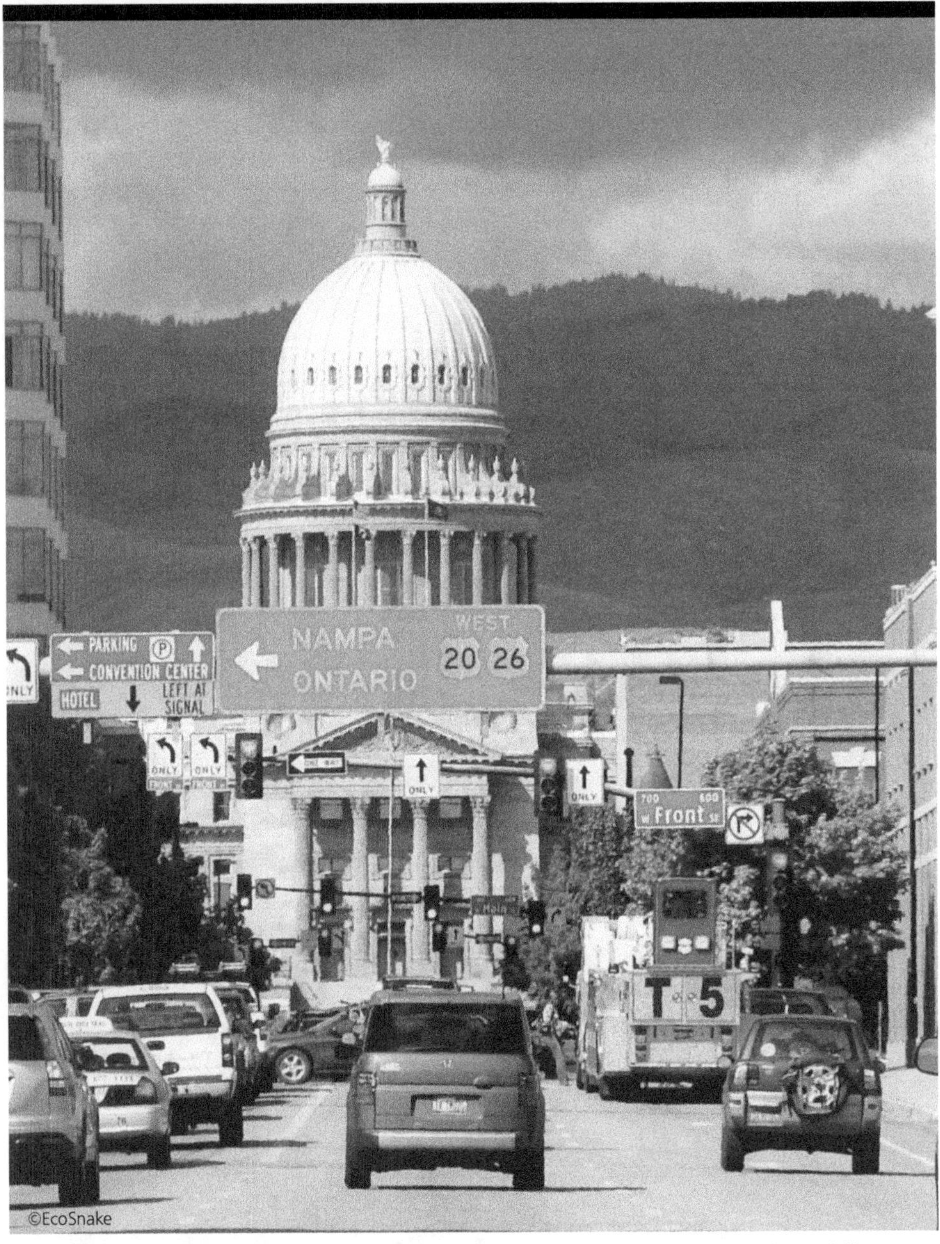

Idaho's Capitol fronts the Boise Foothills. A vibrant downtown and Foothills conservation are keys to sustainable growth.

Growing

SMART

by David Webb

From the vital urban core of downtown Boise to future modes of transportation, a common theme emerges from this collection of essays. There is a need for "smart" strategies to sustain our urban experience, whether it applies to the redevelopment of urban decay along the Orchard and Emerald Street corridors or the proliferation of exurbs being carved out of green fields. As noted in the preceding chapters, urban growth can drastically change our community's landscapes for either better or worse, and greatly affect our temporal ideas of growth and planning. Smart growth is not only essential to the health and well-being of a community, but also is an important factor in the quality of life a city offers. It is what distinguishes a good city from a great one. Smart growth is essentially a methodology; it centers on the relationship between housing, business, transportation and preservation. The successful relationship of these four characteristics comes together to produce a mixed-use development. For that to exist, the emerging complexities of urban sprawl and impractical development have to be tamed. The method of community planning for smart, sustainable living places the emphasis on a mixture of uses in a relatively small space.

Future development should reflect a complimentary use of space and resources, much like the corner of 8th and Idaho in downtown Boise, where mixed-use development incorporates many of the fundamental "smart" necessities. Shops, restaurants, offices and nearby residential accommodations comprise a mixed-use environment that makes it a vibrant and sustainable place. A well-organized neighborhood of this caliber builds on the premise of narrow streets and the revitalization of existing infrastructure, along with large, pedestrian-friendly spaces for residents to socialize. Eighth and Idaho is also a testament to preservation. Many of the buildings on the corner have been used for decades due to preservation efforts by their owners and by the city. The functioning layout of 8th Street gives Boise a template for smart growth. In contrast, increasing urban sprawl and poorly planned living environments pose challenges—longer commutes, a stressed infrastructure and the loss not only of open space, but also of historical context.

Preservation

Preservation is certainly not solely the practice of saving historic architecture or open space. In areas like the Central Bench, development in other parts of the city has left the area a disinvested community of empty storefronts and neglected infrastructure. Traffic crams the streets and abandoned buildings wait for tenants. Preservation can also mean reinvesting in a community like the Central Bench. The City of Boise has initiated the Blueprint Boise process designed to update the current Comprehensive Plan. Blueprint Boise acknowledges the impact that growth has on our current community and proposes several specific plans and/or strategies for managing future expansion. Among the plans considered are some specifically targeted at the need for reinvestment in our disinvested areas to, as Blueprint states, "promote the revitalization of underutilized existing centers over time." These areas are the greyfields of Boise, the abandoned (but still functional) and neglected building spaces left to sit unoccupied and scarcely managed by their owners.

Another goal in Blueprint Boise would "encourage existing single-use centers to incorporate a greater mix of compatible uses, such as offices and housing, through infill, adaptive reuse, or redevelopment." Policy changes are required to accomplish this goal, along with the cooperation of developers, builders and investors who could financially benefit from reinvestment strategies. Because greyfields are generally commercially oriented, codes that would allow existing structures to be converted into high-density residential dwellings are complicated. There is no magic wand that can instantly allow for such adaptation of greyfields. However, the Boise's Comprehensive Plan is a good start.

Not only does preservation apply to the developed parts of the community, but it also relates to the open spaces we have come to enjoy. Today, planned communities such as Avimor and The Cliffs (formerly Hammer Flat) are poised for development. On paper, both developments look sustainable. Both have mixed-use, baseline modes of operation and appeal to consumers as planned communities. Homes, businesses and recreational opportunities formulate a cornerstone methodology for both. From a growth pattern standpoint, both planned communities contribute to sprawl outside the city's area of impact. Though smart planning is incorporated into Avimor and The Cliffs, the main issue against both has been open space preservation. With the Black Cliffs and Highway 21 as its foundation, The Cliffs is planned for a plateau east of Boise, a piece of open space valued for wildlife habitat within close proximity to the city. The idea that this beautiful piece of prime real estate will someday be platted with homes and businesses stirs an ardent push by some for its preservation. Avimor, on the other hand, is located northwest of Boise and miles from the city limits. Primarily planted in alfalfa, the cozy valley once offered passers-by a view of deer and at times, antelope and elk.

Both developments lie outside Boise's jurisdiction—they are beyond Boise's area of impact, but still affect the city through the need for transportation and other services. Essentially, the county determines decisions about property use outside of the city. Avimor and The Cliffs have the approval of Ada County; both met the legal requirements. Avimor is in the process of building homes, but The Cliffs has not reached that point. Legally, the growth that Boise has seen over the last several years has the right to exist. Current codes do not prevent building and sprawl from continuing. However, the recent use of easements and financial incentives for farm and ranch owners to keep their properties in agricultural use may be one strategy to stem the loss of open space, meshing rural development deals with urban needs. (The developers sold the land where The Cliffs was planned to the City of Boise as this publication went to press.)

Transportation

Boise is losing its battle with traffic congestion. With growth that has occurred outside the city, roads in and around Boise are clogged with commuters, a pattern experienced by other urban areas. It appears from the multitude of orange cones and the "Pardon Us For The Inconvenience" construction signs of the Ada County Highway District that efforts are being made to alleviate this problem. But can the issue be successfully addressed simply by improving existing roads? More asphalt doesn't necessarily resolve traffic congestion. The valley is beginning to understand the costs of such a development strategy. Plans to accommodate traffic flow are best solved by smart growth, which utilizes the full potential of a mass transit system. Currently, Boise's transit system is inadequate for the size of the community. Valley Regional Transit has limited options to update the system and provide for an attractive alternative to personal transportation. Funding is a critical issue for VRT and mass transit in general. Additional funds are required to improve the system. One solution may be a local option tax or the issuance of municipal bonds to fund transportation projects. A local option tax is a plausible solution. An extra fraction of one cent in local sales tax could be used to upgrade Boise's transit system. For this option to work, the Idaho State Legislature would first have to grant municipalities like Boise the authority that resort towns like McCall and Sun Valley already have. Once allowed by the Legislature, citizens of the city or town would vote on the new tax, which would require a supermajority (two-thirds) vote. The local option would empower the citizens of Boise to choose whether or not this solution is right for them.

Additional strategies for combating transportation issues are outlined in the "Greenhouse Gas Reduction Strategies for Boise" report. Appointed by Mayor Dave Beiter, six prominent community members make up the Climate Protection Program Advisory Committee, whose goal is to "assist in the development of greenhouse gas reduction strategies..." The committee's July 2008 report provides some viable strategies. In addition to the adoption of a local option tax, it is recommended that "transit-oriented development," which places residential infrastructure in proximity to areas of work and traffic corridors, be adopted. The plan considers providing incentives for residential dwellings to create higher-density living areas that "support transit along traffic corridors." These dwelling units would be near the mass transit infrastructure, which would increase the ridership of city's public transit system and revitalize areas along the routes. This recommendation also endorses "Location Efficient Mortgages" that would encourage lenders to offer mortgages to commuters who chose to live closer to work. This financial tool could mitigate the need to live further from the city because of more affordable housing options. The committee also recommended "employer alternative transportation programs" that target Boise building owners, developers and other city employers by providing incentives for "density bonuses," "zoning changes" and "expanding downtown parking districts."

Limits of Growth

Sprawl, as defined in *The American Heritage Dictionary*, is "to spread out in a staggering or disordered fashion." Certainly, the key term is "disordered." Today, an array of homes, businesses, roads and mass development reach across Boise and the surrounding areas. "Disordered" sprawl has bled into the valley's open spaces. During the early days of Boise's history, growth simply occurred. Towns essentially grew in convenient locations, a pattern evident in many of the West's early settlements. However, with the advent of the automobile and without the proper planning of space, resources and housing alternatives, sprawl has developed. For Boise, this has gobbled up much of our open space and swelled the present city. Growth has choked out the individuality of places like Collister, Ustick and the areas around Orchard and Emerald and replaced that with a municipal backdrop of uninterrupted homes and businesses. Boise has seen great changes in the physical layout and structure of its neighborhoods. Collister and Ustick were once agricultural landscapes—open spaces of fields and orchards considered by their residents as townships apart from Boise. They were almost entirely farming communities, shipping fruit and other agricultural commodities to the metropolis via rail line. Named after their prominent patrons, these two small towns offer Boise a unique and individualized stamp on its history. Early Ustick and Collister point to a picture of what once was—a bustling hub of mixed-use development and a heritage of smart planning based on a philosophy that contrasts to sprawl.

The introduction of the trolley system (mass transit) and later the automobile led to the beginning of sprawl, eventually causing one-time outskirt villages like Ustick and Collister to lose their identities. As commute times into larger municipalities like Boise were shortened, more residents migrated out of the city. Once the automobile replaced much of the nation's public transit options, growth of unexpected proportions flooded into the country's open spaces. Boise was not immune to this expansion, leading to what we now see—homes, businesses and development of all kinds filling the Boise Valley. The remains of our farming townships are pushed further west and privately held open space near the city is being sold for developments.

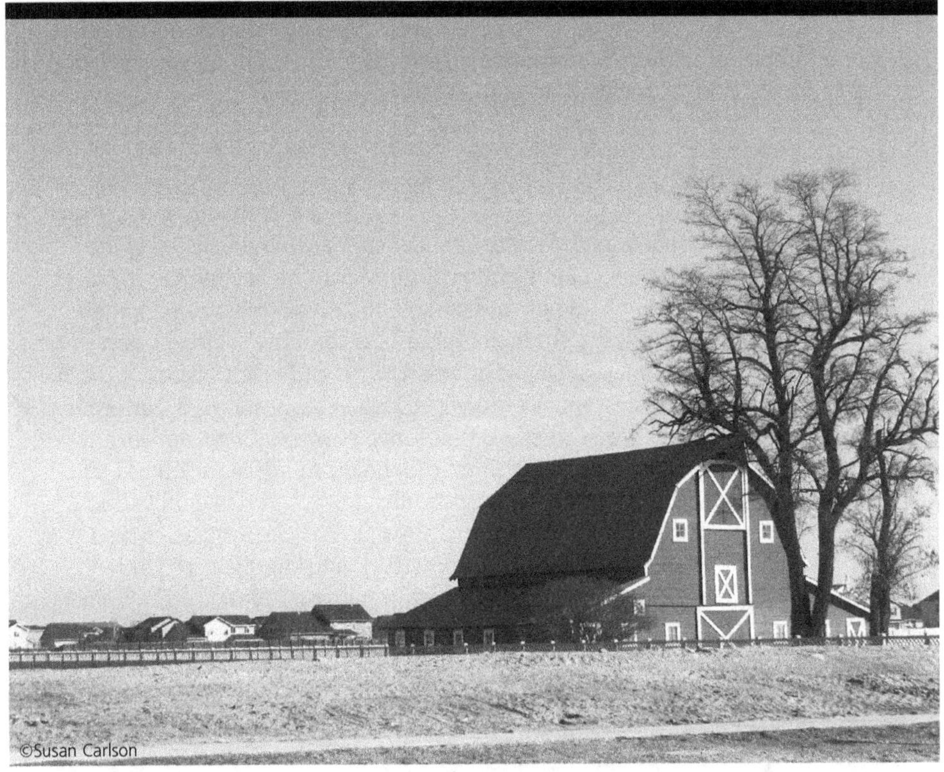

©Susan Carlson

A subdivision consumes farmland near Meridian in West Ada County.

Sprawl has its reasons. Once understood by municipal governments and citizens, Boise can work in concert with its residents to enable smart growth planning, which can potentially quell or mitigate future sprawl. Its resolution starts with simple, yet effective strategies. Boise has an inventory of high- and low-income housing options, but insufficient middle-income housing opportunities. The downtown area currently employs approximately 40,000 workers, according to a Capital City Development Corporation estimate. Only 2,000 downtown residential dwellings exist. The CCDC has published a "Workforce Housing Policy" with recommendations and strategies to address this issue. By establishing more mid-range housing options, life in downtown could outweigh the conveniences of suburban living.

Much depends on a citizenry that is informed about the impacts of growth on transportation, pollution and habitat preservation. Education about the benefits of smart growth is key to implementing effective solutions for Boise. Without smart strategies to guide to our city's future, issues such as transportation and preservation will challenge Boise's livability as we move forward. This collection of essays provides readers with a context to understand not only the rich heritage of our city, but also the challenges confronting neighbors and city officials in their quest to make this the "most livable city in America." The essays are filled with optimism about the citizens who care about their neighborhoods and get involved to shape our future community. Today's activists and developers follow the traditions and vision articulated by their predecessors who built neighborhoods like Collister and made Boise the cultural and economic center of the valley The students' essays reveal how investigating one's environment can lead to significant insight and foster a commitment to help Boise realize its vision.

● ● ●

David Webb is a 2001 home-school graduate. He will graduate from Boise State in May 2010 with a BA in political science. He plans to pursue a law degree after graduation. He was a candidate for a seat on the Boise City Council in 2009.

What are the most important aspects of a "livable" city?

"Aspects of a livable city include efficient transportation modes, open space preservation and sustainable policies for future growth. To be successful, a city's political culture and value proposition(s) should align together to promote these three aspects of a livable city."

Sources

Ch. 1: Boise Builds a Streetcar

"Bondsmen Buy Traction Line." *Idaho Statesman*. 1928. Vertical file. Boise Public Library.

"Caldwell." Idaho Press-Tribune. March 12, 2008.

"Cars Killed Valley Trollies." *Boise West*. February 15, 1978.

"Economic and Social Benefits of Vintage/Heritage Trolley and Streetcar Lines." *APTA Streetcar and Heritage Trolley Site*. www.heritagetrolley.com/Overview.

Fischler, Stanley I. *Moving Millions*. New York: Harper and Row Publishers, Inc., 1979.

Grote, Tom. "Remember? Buried rails recall a bygone era." *Idaho Statesman*. October 13, 1980.

Hart, Arthur. "New-fangled streetcars found popularity quickly in Boise." *Idaho Statesman*. August 23, 1892.

Hoffman, Nathaniel. "Training Wheels." *Boise Weekly*. August 13, 2008; "Boise streetcar route proposed." Idaho Press-Tribune. September 8, 2008.

Holle, Gena. *The San Diego Trolley*. Glendale: Interurban Press, 1990.

Jones, William. *Mile-High Trolley*s. Denver: National Railway Historical Society, Inc., 1975.

Johnson, Jordan and Amanda Roberg. "Trolley House". Boise Architecture Project. www.boisearchitecture.org/section.php?id=288.

Krueger, Dr. Phillip M. "It's time for Boiseans to jump aboard the light rail train." *Idaho Statesman*. July 8, 2008.

Newman, Peter, and Jeffrey Kenworthy. *Sustainability and Cities: Overcoming Automobile Dependence*. Washington D.C.: Island Press, 1999.

Pearson, Margaret. "Pioneer Boiseans Rode to Town On Old-Tie 'Toonerville'." *Idaho Statesman*. July 13, 1952.

Sewell, Cynthia. "Boise leaders raise streetcar concerns." *Idaho Statesman*. June 14, 2009.

Sewell, Cynthia. "Downtown Boise streetcar plan on track." *Idaho Statesman*. May 27, 2009.

Sewell, Cynthia. "Will Boise hear the clang of a trolley again?" *Idaho Statesman*. June 9, 2008.

Thompson, Richard. *Images of Rail: Portland's Streetcars*. Chicago: Arcadia Publishing, 2006.

"Traction Line Will Be Sold." *Idaho Statesman*. 1928. Vertical file. Boise Public Library.

"Tram." *Wikipedia, the free encyclopedia*. 2009. www.en.wikipedia.org/wiki/Tram.

"Why a Streetcar?" *Boise Streetcar*. WordPress, 2009.

Woodward, Tim. "Ask Tim: Boise Bench's historic trolley will rise from ashes." *Idaho Statesman*. March 22, 2009.

Woodward, Tim. "Woodward: Can we afford to scrap the trolley?" *Idaho Statesman*. March 1, 2009.

Ch. 2: Saving the Warehouse

Articles on Boise Businesses. MS0310. Idaho State Historical Library and Archives, Boise.

Boise and Idaho Express Fast Freight Co. Waybill 1865. MS2/0017. Idaho State Historical Library and Archives, Boise.

Boise Business firms. MS2/0683. Idaho State Historical Library and Archives, Boise. Booth Furniture and Lemp's merchants. MS2/0501. Idaho State Historical Library and Archives, Boise.

Chamber of Commerce. MS0394. Idaho State Historical Library and Archives, Boise. Financial documents relating to location of Depot in Boise. MS 2/0026. Idaho State Historical Library and Archives, Boise.

Food Products Co. of Idaho. MS0278. Idaho State Historical Library and Archives, Boise.

Kratville, William. *Golden Rails*. Omaha: Barnham Press, 1965.

Records of General Merchant Stores in Boise. MS0573. Idaho State Historical Library and Archives, Boise.

Rim on railroads in Boise. MS2/0803. Idaho State Historical Library and Archives, Boise.

Planmakers Inc., *The History of Boise's 8th Street Marketplace*. Boise: Planmakers.

Potter, Janet Greenstein. *Great American Railroad Stations*. New York: John Wiles and Sons, Inc., 1996.

Interviews

Bertram, John. April 6, 2006.

Everhart, John. April 7, 2006.

McLeod, Theresa. April 19, 2006.

Ch. 3: Creating Collister

"36th and Hill Road due for overhaul." *Idaho Statesman*, March 22, 2005.

Ada County Platt Map. Map G4273 .S1 A3 1917 .In8. Idaho State Historical Library and Archives. Boise.

Bernard, Joshua. "Boise, The City of Trees." May 3, 2006. Office of the Historian, City of Boise. www.boisehistory.com

Casner, Nick, and Valerie Kiesig. *Trolley: Boise Valley's Electric Railroad 1891-1928*. Boise: Black Canyon Communications, 2002.

"Collister Elementary celebrates new sculpture in Catalpa Park." *Idaho Statesman*. Jan. 28, 2005.

"Collister Neighborhood Association." *Collister Neighborhood Comprehensive Plan*. 9 Jan. 2004. www.collistercna.org.

"Collister residents hone plan." *Idaho Statesman*. February 28, 2006.

"Collister neighbors worry about traffic." *Idaho Statesman*. January 28, 2005.

"Collister residents have nearly finished neighborhood plan." *Idaho Statesman*. June 21, 2006.

"Death Claims Dr. Collister, Boise Pioneer". *Idaho Statesman*. October 19, 1935.

"Interurban electric trains catered to pleasure, business." *Idaho Statesman*. January 9, 2007.

Interview

Keener, Edward. Collister Neighborhood Association Regional Representative. April 10, 2007.

Ch. 4: Ustick on the Brink of Place

Beatly, Timothy, and Kristy Manning. *The Ecology of Place: Planning for Environment, Economy and Community* . Washington, D.C.: Island Press, 1997.

Casner, Nick, and Valerie Kiesig. *Trolley: Boise Valley's Electric Railroad 1891-1928*.

 Boise: Black Canyon Communications, 2002.

Duany Andres. *Suburban Nation*. New York: North Point Press, 2001.

Duany Andres, Elizabeth Plater-Zyberk, and Jeff Speck, *Suburban Nation: The Rise of Sprawl and the Decline of the American Dream*. New York: North Point Press, 2000.

Engwicht, David. *Reclaiming our Cities and Towns: Better Living With Less Traffic* New York: New Society Publishers, 1993.

"Five-Mile and Ustick Survey." Boise State University, Department of Public Policy, Fall 1999.

Hayden, Delores. *The Power of Place: Urban Landscapes as Public History*. MIT Press, 1995.

Idaho Traction Company, "Interurban Time Tables." Nov. 16, 1913.

Jackson, Kenneth T. *The Crabgrass Frontier* . New York: Oxford University Press, 2000.

Johncox, Martin S. "Push to Preserve Ustick's Past Puts Districts on Trial." *Idaho Statesman*. Vertical file. Boise Public Library.

Kunstler, James Howard. *Geography of Nowhere: The Rise and Decline of America's Man-Made Landscape*. New York: Free Press, 1994.

"Like A Weed: Articles of Incorporation Filed Yesterday for a Bank." *Idaho Statesman*. July 31, 1907.

Marshall, Alex. *How Cities Work: Suburban Sprawl and the Roads Not Taken*. Austin, TX: University of Texas Press, 2000.

"Our View: ACHD, Council Shame Themselves Over Ustick Road." *Idaho Statesman*. Oct. 8, 2005

Sewell, Cynthia. "City Wants Fewer Lanes to Preserve Neighborhood." *Idaho Statesman*. Aug. 2, 2005.

Sewell,Cynthia. "Ustick Road Compromise Falls Apart," *Idaho Statesman*. Sept. 7, 2005.

Szold, Terry S., and Armando Carbonell. eds., *Smart Growth: Form and Consequences*. Cambridge, MA: Lincoln Institute of Land Policy, 2002.

"The West Valley Community Center Plan: Goals, Objectives and Policies."

Weatherby, James B., and Randy Stapilus. *Governing Idaho: Politics, People and Power*. Caldwell, ID: Caxton Press, 2005.

Woodward, Tim. "Village of Ustick May Yet Find Its Place in History." *Idaho Statesman*. Aug. 19, 1997.

Interviews:

Alloway, Don. West Valley Neighborhood Association board member. October 17, 2005.

Clymens, Gladys. Ustick townsite resident and former WVNA board Member. Sept. 28, 2005.

McKibbin, Sherry. Head Professor, Idaho Urban Research Design Center. October 2000.

Ch. 5: Scoop Leeburn's Lost City

Hernandez, Jennifer. "Royal Plaza, 1112 Main St." *The Boise Weekly*. www.boiseweekly.com/boise/royal-plaza-1112-main-st/Content?oid=935201.

"Historic American Buildings Survey." Heritage Conservation and Recreation Service, Department of the Interior. www.lcweb2.loc.gov/pnp/habshaer/id/id0000/id0016/data/id0016.pdf.

Woodward, Tim. "Woodward: All that's left of a Boise treasure." *Idaho Statesman*. www.idahostatesman.com/Woodward/story/890327.html.

Ch. 6: Urban Crossroads

American Institute of Architects: Idaho Chapter. Boise R/UDAT. October 11-14, 1985. Boise.

Arrington, Leonard J. *History of Idaho*. 1, 2 vols. Moscow, ID: University of Idaho Press, 1994.

"Boise". Outdoor Idaho. Designing Idaho: Some Shining Examples. http://idahoptv.org/outdoors/shows/designingidaho/boise.html.

Digital Sanborn Maps 1867-1970. Proquest. http://sanborn.umi.com.libproxy.boisestate.edu/.

Hart, Arthur. *The Boiseans: At Home*. Boise: Historic Boise, Incorporated, 1985.

Idaho Business Review. 1984-Current. Vertical file. Boise Public Library.

Idaho Statesman. 1864-Current. Vertical file. Boise Public Library.

MacGregor, Carol Lynn. *Boise, Idaho 1882-1910: Prosperity in Isolation*. Missoula, MT: Mountain Publishing Company, 2006.

Shallat, Todd. *Ethnic Landmarks: Ten Historic Places that Define the City of Trees*. Boise: Boise City Office of the Historian, 2007.

"Urban Renewal District History." *CCDC Boise*. Capital City Development Corp. www.ccdcboise.com/AboutCCDC/History.aspx.

Vertical files. Boise Public Library

Vertical files. Idaho State Historical Library and Archives

Wells, Merle W. *Boise, An Illustrated History*. Woodland Hills, CA: Windsor Publications, 1982.

Zimmer Gunsul Frasca Partnership, et. al, *Boise Downtown Urban Design Plan*,. 1, 2 vols. Boise: March 1986.

Interviews

Howell, Ken. Owner, Parklane Management Company, LLC. October 2009.

Kushlan, Phil. Executive Director, Capital City Development Corporation (CCDC). September 8, 2009.

Neill, J.M. Historian. October 16, 2009.

Sander, Karen. Executive Director, Downtown Boise Association. June 25, 2009.

Sheldon, Pam. Contracts Manager, Capital City Development Corporation (CCDC). October 23, 2009

Ch. 7: Revitalizing the Bench

Beaver, Carolyn. "Oregon Trail Crossed the Bench." *Idaho Statesman*. Sept. 6, 1978.

Chambers, Albert M. "Charter Stands in Way: Extension of City Limits to Include Bench Areas Seen as Gradual Process." *Idaho Statesman*. Sept. 1,1960.

Duany, Andres, and Elizabeth Plater-Zyberk, and Jeff Speck. "The American Transportation Mess." *Suburban Nation: The Rise of Sprawl and the Decline of the American Dream*. New York: North Point Press, 2000.

Duany, Andres, and Elizabeth Plater-Zyberk, and Jeff Speck. "What is To Be Done." *Suburban Nation: The Rise of Sprawl and the Decline of the American Dream*. New York: North Point Press, 2000.

Duany, Andres, and Elizabeth Plater-Zyberk, and Jeff Speck. "The Physical Creation of Society." *Suburban Nation: The Rise of Sprawl and the Decline of the American Dream*. New York: North Point Press, 2000.

Congress for the New Urbanism. "Greyfields into Goldfields: From Failing Shopping Centers to Great Neighborhoods." Feb. 2001.

Hester, Johnny. "Reinventing Boise: Changing Influences on Boise's Growth Pattern as Exhibited through Maps, 1863-1930." Boise State University. www.boisestate.edu/history/cityhistorian/atlas_city/atlas_reinvent/atlas_reinvent.html#/.

Jacobs, Allan. "An Introduction to Great Streets." *Great Streets*. 1993.

Martin, Marion. "Old-Timers to Picnic; Memories of Boise's Bench." *Idaho Statesman*. Aug. 10, 1962.

Volkert, Lora. "CCDC Considers Expansion Outside of Downtown Area in Boise." *Idaho Business Review*. Oct. 15, 2007.

Webb, Jay. "Minutes of April 4, 2007." *Boise City Hearing Examiner*. 2007. Boise City Planning & Development Services. www.cityofboise.org/

"Bench Group Okehs Proposal for City Annexation; Collister Residents Give Strong Refusal to Program." *Idaho Statesman*. Jan. 30, 1959.

Interviews

Bounyavong, Mock. Chiang Mai House, Owner. June 21, 2009.

Chan, C.C. Wok-Inn, Owner. June 23, 2009.

Johnson, Joan. Boise City Planning & Development–Neighborhood Planner. June 23, 2009.

Kurtagic, Dusanka. Bosnia-Express, Owner. 20 June 2009.

McKibbin, Sherry. Head Professor, Idaho Urban Research Design Center. June 18, 2009.

Norman. Neighboring homeowner. June 22, 2009.

Perlman, Rainey. Area resident. June 24, 2009.

Sorensen, Andrea. Wireless Toys, Owner. June 23, 2009.

Ta, Hoa. Oriental Market, Owner. June 21, 2009.

Ch. 8: Bus Rapid Transit

APTA Streetcar and Heritage Trolley Site. Sept. 9, 2009. SeashoreTrolley Museum. Kennebunkport, Maine. www.heritagetrolley.com.

Eberle, David. Lecture. July 7, 2009.

Luft, Amy. (CIM) Communities in Motion pamphlet and handouts. COMPASS. July 9, 2009.

Martinez, Kendra. "Shuttle service may expand: Meridian, Nampa riders make test project a success." *Idaho Statesman*. June 17, 2001.

Porticha, Shelley, and Gloria Ohland. *Urban Idyll: A Case Study of the Portland Streetcar; Street SmartStreetcars and Cities in the Twenty-First Century*. Oakland, CA: Reconnecting America.

Schrag, Zachary. "Urban Mass Transit In The United States." *EH.Net Encyclopedia*, edited by Robert Whaples. May 7, 2002. www.eh.net/encyclopedia/article/schrag.mass.transit.us.

Shallat, Todd. Lecture. July 7, 2009.

"Working with CCDC & Boise City." Capital City Development Corp. 2009. www.ccdcboise.com/InformationForDevelopers/WorkingWithCCDCAndBoise City.aspx.

Wood, David, and Gloria Ohland. *Four Case Studies*. Oakland, CA: Reconnecting America.

Interviews

Charles Trainor, Director of Planning for COMPASS. Sept. 17, 2009.

Ingram, Karalee. Petty Officer. July 9, 2009.

Kathleen Lacey. Boise City Planning and Development Department. Sept. 13, 2009; January 21, 2010.

Ch. 9: Scaling The Cliffs

"Decade of Ada County growth slowing; planners look for next wave." 2News.TV. www.2news.tv/news/16748116.html.

"Wildlife Mitigation Plan." Savetheplateau.org. July 28, 2009. www.Savetheplateau.org/index2.html.

Scholten, Jerry. "Hammer Flat Community Planned Development draft." *Save the Plateau*. 2005. www.savetheplateau.org/Scholten%20Draft%20.pdf.

"Urban growth boundary." Metro Regional Government. 2009. www.oregonmetro.gov/index.cfm/go/by.web/id=277.

Van Vooren, A. "Hammer Flat Development ." *Save the Plateau*. 2005. www.savetheplateau.org/Fish_Game_Cmnts.pdf.

Interviews

Epeldi, Sandy. Author *Boise Climbs*. July 15, 2009.

Fedigan, Brian. President, Boise Climber Alliance. July 12, 2009.

Franden, John. ACHD Commissioner. September 16, 2009.

Golden, Pam. IDT Development & Access Management Engineer. September 17, 2009.

Johnson, Tucker. President, Skyline Development. September 29, 2009; January 25, 2010

Perkins, Dusty. Instructor, College of Western Idaho. July14, 2009.

Sewall, Cynthia. *Idaho Statesman*. August 3, 2006.

Tilman, Fred. Ada County Commissioner. October 11, 2009; January 14, 2010.

Zuzel, Michael. Assistant to the Mayor. October 8, 2009; January 6, 2010.

Ch. 10: More like Avimor?

Baun, Charles. "Avimor Wildlife Mitigation Plan." *Avimor*. Dec. 2006. SunCor ID, Inc.,
www.avimor.com/residents/files/wildlife-mitigation-plan.pdf.

Carson, Pat. "Your Business Community-Your Treasure Valley Business Community: Accomplishments
and Promotions...." *Idaho Statesman*. May 2009. www.infoweb.newsbank.com.

Dey, Ken. "Regulators Deny Deal—Commission Strikes Down $4.3 Million Proposal Between Developer
and Idaho Power." *Idaho Statesman*. May 25, 2007. www.infoweb.newsbank.com.

Sewell, Cythia. "Boise's Objection to Homes Dismissed." *Idaho Statesman*. Nov. 10, 2006.
www.infoweb.newsbank.com.

Sewell, Cynthia. "Star Enters Legal Battle Between Boise and Ada County over Avimor." *Idaho
Statesman*. Sept. 2, 2006. www.infoweb.newsbank.com.

Taunton, Robert. "Avimor and SunCor Development." President of SunCor Idaho Inc. Lecture. July 7,
2009.

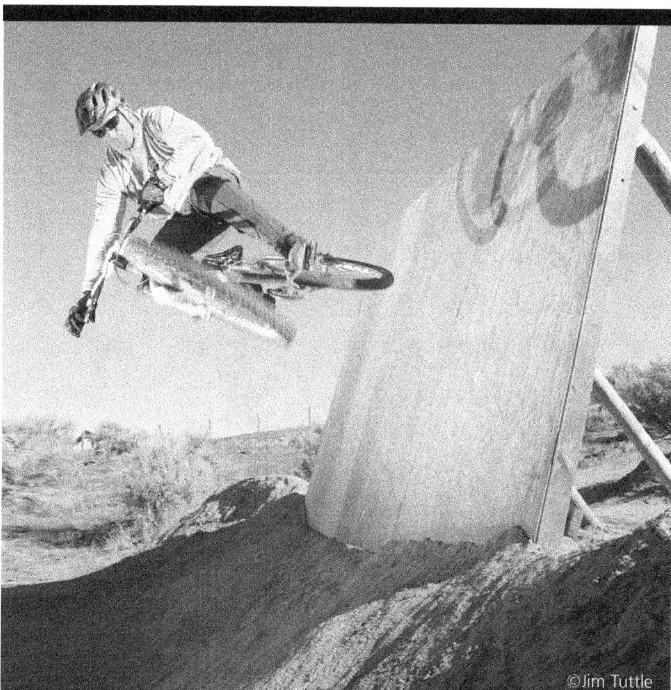

Biking in the Boise Foothills. Recreationalists think biking
and hiking make Boise a livable place.

Boise State University

Boise State, with an enrollment of nearly 19,000 students, is a progressive student-focused university dedicated to excellence in teaching, innovative research, leadership development and community service. Its students benefit from an emphasis on the undergraduate experience, including public affairs research as demonstrated by the student papers in this publication.

With record student enrollment, new academic buildings, additional degree programs and an expanding research portfolio, it is no coincidence that in 2009 Boise State was ranked by *U.S. News & World Report* among the nation's "top up-and-coming schools." With Idaho's fastest-growing research program, Boise State is in the midst of a transformation that builds on its traditional teaching strengths while expanding its capabilities in research and scholarly activity. This evolution reflects the integral role that Boise State plays in contributing to the quality of life in the Treasure Valley and beyond.

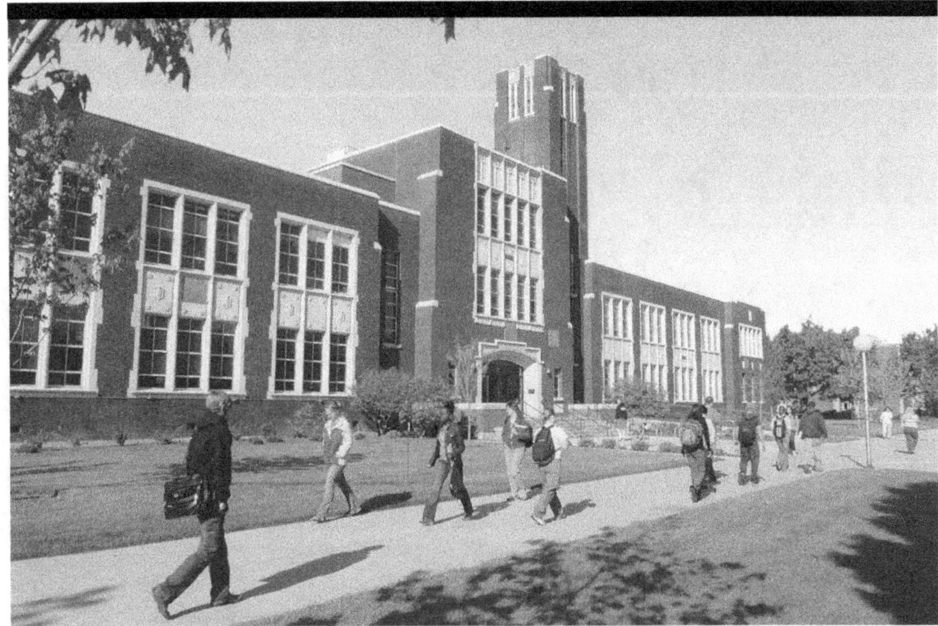

www.ingramcontent.com/pod-product-compliance
Lightning Source LLC
Chambersburg PA
CBHW060943050726
47592CB00003B/1089